ELVIS PRESLEY
Fighting for the Right to Rock

REBELS WITH A CAUSE

ELVIS PRESLEY

Fighting for the Right to Rock

Enslow Publishing
101 W. 23rd Street
Suite 240
New York, NY 10011
USA

enslow.com

John Micklos Jr.

Published in 2018 by Enslow Publishing, LLC.
101 W. 23rd Street, Suite 240, New York, NY 10011

Library of Congress Cataloging-in-Publication Data

Names: Micklos, John.
Title: Elvis Presley : fighting for the right to rock / by John Micklos Jr.
Description: New York : Enslow Publishing, [2018] | Series: Rebels with a cause |
Includes bibliographical references and index. | Audience: Grades 7-12.
Identifiers: LCCN 2017027306 | ISBN 9780766092587 (library bound) | ISBN
9780766095496 (paperback)
Subjects: LCSH: Presley, Elvis, 1935-1977—Juvenile literature. | Rock musicians—
United States—Biography—Juvenile literature.
Classification: LCC ML3930.P73 M52 2018 | DDC 782.42166092 [B] —dc23
LC record available at https://lccn.loc.gov/2017027306

Printed in China

To Our Readers: We have done our best to make sure all website addresses in this
book were active and appropriate when we went to press. However, the author
and the publisher have no control over and assume no liability for the material
available on those websites or on any websites they may link to. Any comments or
suggestions can be sent by email to customerservice@enslow.com.

Portions of this book originally appeared in *Elvis Presley: "I Want to Entertain
People"* by John Micklos Jr.

Photo Credits: Cover, p. 3 Archive Photos/Moviepix/Getty Images; p. 7 CBS Photo
Archive/Getty Images; pp. 13, 24, 51, 69, 82, 84, 94 Michael Ochs Archive/Getty
Images; pp. 16, 19 RB/Redferns/Getty Images; p. 29 Gavin Hellier/robertharding/
Getty Images; p. 32 Colin Escott/Michael Ochs Archives/Getty Images; pp. 38, 45,
62, 75, 78 Bettmann/Getty Images; pp. 40, 54-55 Hulton Archive/Archive Photos/
Getty Images; p. 50 John Springer Collection/Corbis Historical/Getty Images; p.
59 Pictorial Parade/Archive Photos/Getty Images; p. 90 National Archives/Hulton
Archive/Getty Images; p. 99 Ronald C. Modra/Sports Imagery/Hulton Archive/
Getty Images; p. 103 Blank Archives/Hulton Archive/Getty Images; p. 105 Richard
Howard/The LIFE Images Collection/Getty Images; p. 106 Donald Kravitz/Getty
Images; interior pages graphic element Eky Studio/Shutterstock.com.

CONTENTS

INTRODUCTION

B y today's standards, Elvis Presley's performances seem mild. He did not descend from the rafters like Lady Gaga. No fireworks exploded. He remained fully clothed. Still, screams erupted from the audience as Elvis Presley strode onstage to perform his hit song "Don't Be Cruel" for *The Ed Sullivan Show* on September 9, 1956. Although his performance was relatively subdued, every movement "evoked screams" from the crowd.[1]

A record audience of some sixty million people watched Elvis on *The Ed Sullivan Show* that night.[2] The rock and roll rebel rocked the nation.

What made this accomplishment even more amazing was the fact that Ed Sullivan had previously declared he would never invite Elvis on his wildly popular show. Sullivan did not approve of Elvis's hip swinging and rock-and-roll singing. "He is not my cup of tea," Sullivan was quoted as saying.[3]

Elvis Presley first appeared on *The Ed Sullivan Show* in September 1956, shaking his hips and strumming his guitar for an audience of sixty million people. He appeared on the show two more times and is shown here during his October 1956 performance.

Elvis did not need Sullivan's help. Elvis had four number-one hits in 1956: "Heartbreak Hotel"; "I Want You, I Need You, I Love You"; "Don't Be Cruel/Hound Dog"; and "Love Me Tender."

"Heartbreak Hotel" opened the floodgates. On April 21, the song reached number one on *Billboard Magazine's* chart of hot music hits. "It marked Elvis's transition from a local southern sensation to a national phenomenon," *Billboard* later wrote. "The king of rock and roll had just ascended to his throne."[4]

Sullivan realized he could not stop Elvis from becoming a star. Grudgingly, he spoke to Elvis's manager, Colonel Tom Parker, about having Elvis appear on his show, not once but three times. Parker demanded—and got—Elvis a fee of $50,000 for the appearances. That was far more than any other act could command at that time.[5]

Young listeners loved Elvis and the new form of music he represented; girls fell for his sexy looks, and boys started to wear their hair slicked back like Elvis. Many parents and critics were less thrilled. They found Elvis's music too wild and his hip-swinging vulgar. His wild performances earned him the nickname "Elvis the Pelvis," which Elvis found offensive.[6]

Concern continued to mount. Indeed, on his third appearance on *The Ed Sullivan Show*, on January 6, 1957, he was filmed only from the waist up. That way, his swinging hips wouldn't offend anyone.[7]

Not all parents found Elvis objectionable, however. Indeed, some television historians believe Elvis's appearances on *The Ed Sullivan Show* helped "bridge the generation gap for Elvis's acceptance into the mainstream."[8] As he introduced Elvis's final number, Sullivan himself said, "This is a real decent, fine boy. We've never had a pleasanter experience on our show with a big name than we've had with you."[9]

Over the years, Elvis's career evolved from rock-and-roll rebel to movie star to soldier to ballad crooner to Las Vegas performer. His body evolved from svelte to bloated. Through it all, he retained legions of fans. His meteoric rise to stardom was made all the more remarkable by his truly humble beginnings.

1

A Legend Is Born

Elvis Presley was almost a twin. Around 4:00 a.m. on January 8, 1935, Gladys Presley gave birth in her two-room house in Tupelo, Mississippi. The baby, named Jesse Garon, was born dead. Half an hour later, at 4:35 a.m., a second baby, Elvis Aaron, arrived.

Gladys believed that "when one twin died, the one that lived got all the strength of both."[1] She passed that belief on to Elvis, and he remained fascinated with his twin throughout his life.

Growing Up Poor

In 1935, the United States was in the midst of the Great Depression. At the worst point, in 1933, one out of every four workers was unemployed.[2]

Like many other families, the Presleys were poor. Elvis's father, Vernon, had a bad back. This limited his ability to do some jobs. Also, he lacked any ambition or drive. Despite his faults, however, Vernon was very handsome. At the age of seventeen, he met twenty-one-year-old Gladys Love Smith at the First Assembly of God Tabernacle. They immediately fell in love. Within two months, they eloped. They were unprepared. They lacked the $3 fee for the license, and Vernon was not of legal age.[3]

The two young lovers managed to borrow the money for the license. Then, on June 17, 1933, they traveled to a nearby county where no one knew them. Vernon claimed he was twenty-two, and Gladys said she was nineteen.

Gladys had lived a hard life, and life did not get much easier when she married Vernon. "She simply accepted him for what he was: a ravishingly handsome, tenderhearted, unambitious young loafer," wrote Elvis biographer Elaine Dundy.[4]

Perhaps because she had lost her other baby, Gladys felt very protective of Elvis. "She doted on him constantly," recalled longtime friend Lamar Fike, "a smothering kind of affection."[5]

THE GREAT DEPRESSION

Throughout the 1930s, the United States suffered a long economic downturn. Years of bad weather led to poor crop yields in the Midwest. The stock market crashed, and many banks failed. Many people lost all of their savings. People found it hard to find any kind of work. Growing up poor, Elvis lacked fancy food and nice clothes. Partly because of that, when he grew wealthy, Elvis spent lots of money on expensive food, clothes, and cars. But he didn't spend all the money on himself. Elvis was famed for his generosity to his family and friends

Everyone noticed how close Elvis was to his mother. The bond with his hard-drinking, less affectionate father was much less strong.

Life grew even harder for the Presley family after Vernon was arrested in 1937 for check fraud. Vernon spent eight months in prison. While Vernon was in prison, Gladys struggled to keep food on the table for her and Elvis. She had to give up the family's tiny home and move in with relatives.

Mama's Boy

During Vernon's absence, Gladys and Elvis grew even closer. Elvis later recalled, "I was an only child—a very protected and spoiled only child."[6]

Elvis and his mother had pet names for each other. Elvis's included "Ageless", "Naughty", and "Baby". Meanwhile, Elvis called Gladys "Satnin"—the brand name of a lard product. That meant his mama was "chubby, round, and comfortable."[7]

When Elvis and Gladys welcomed Vernon back, Elvis remained shy and restrained around his father. Meanwhile, Vernon and Gladys grew further and further apart. Their love of Elvis held them together.

School Days

Teachers recall Elvis as being quiet and shy. An average student, he did not attract a lot of attention from either teachers or classmates. Sometimes, however, other children taunted Elvis because his father had been in prison and often did not have a job.

Elvis's third-grade class picture shows him standing apart from the other children. His arms were folded, and his hair was neatly combed. He had that familiar pouting smile for which he would later become famous. But, in the picture he seems disconnected from his peers.[8]

By 1942, the United States was fully involved in World War II. Vernon went to northern Mississippi to help build

A two-year-old Elvis poses with his parents, Gladys and Vernon Presley, for a photo in 1937. Presley was an only child and was doted on by his mother, though his father remained distant.

a prisoner of war camp. It would house enemy soldiers captured during the fighting in Europe.

The following year Vernon moved to Memphis, Tennessee. There he worked in a factory that made munitions for the war effort. He returned to Tupelo only on weekends.

While Vernon was gone, Gladys and Elvis kept on with their lives. Meanwhile, young Elvis discovered his real passion: music.

2
Musical Beginnings

From an early age, Elvis was fascinated with music and radio. In fact, he began his public singing career before he was ten years old. On Saturday afternoons, local radio station WELO broadcast "Saturday Jamboree," featuring local talent. Announcer Charlie Boren recalls that Elvis came every Saturday from the time he was about eight years old.

Elvis soon became a regular performer. He sang songs ranging from cowboy tunes to gospel. One favorite was "Old Shep," a heart-wrenching ballad about a boy and his dog.

Over time, Elvis also struck up a friendship with a local musician named Carvel Lee Ausborn, who went by the stage name of Mississippi Slim. Slim toured across the United States playing country music.

Slim had a noontime show on Saturdays on WELO, just before "Saturday Jamboree." His younger brother James went to school with Elvis. "He was crazy about music," James recalled. "That's all he talked about."[1] The boys would walk into town on Saturday, and Elvis would ask Slim to show him some chords.

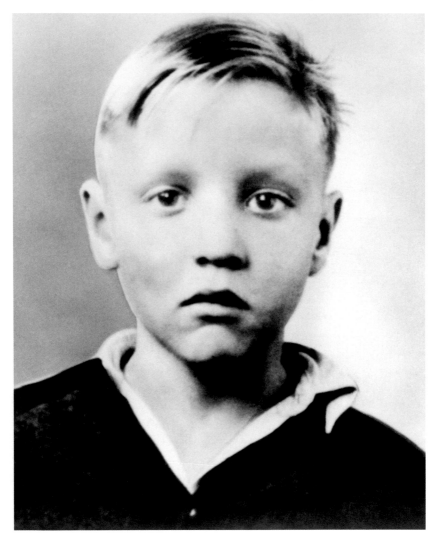

Elvis, photographed here in the 1940s, found music at a young age. His love of song began in church, where the gospel singers wowed him with their talent and uninhibited passion for their music.

A Gospel Singer

Elvis loved the kind of gospel music he heard in church.[2] Elvis often spoke about the role of church music in his development as a singer. He even said that his wild gyrations dated back to watching gospel singers in church.

16

"They're not afraid to move their bodies, and that's where I got it," he said. "When I started singing, I just did what came natural, what they taught me. God is natural."[3]

Changing Fortunes

At the age of ten, Elvis sang in a talent show at the annual fair held in downtown Tupelo. Elvis later recalled his performance in the children's competition. "I wore glasses, no music, and I won, I think it was fifth place in this state talent contest," he said.[4]

Years later, Elvis recalled the event, saying, "I just went out there and started singing. I'd set my heart on singing and nothing in the world could have stopped me from entering the talent contest. I did it all on my own."[5]

FIRST GUITAR

All rock stars have to start somewhere. Elvis Presley's first guitar came from a local hardware store and cost less than $10. Beatle John Lennon learned to play banjo from his mother before later switching to guitar. One of the early electric guitars he used with the Beatles sold at auction in 2015 for more than $2.4 million. Johnny Cash bought his first guitar for $5 in Germany. Keith Richards of the Rolling Stones got his first guitar as a present from his mother around the age of fifteen. He taught himself to play a number of songs, including "That's All Right, Mama" by Elvis Presley.

17

Meanwhile, other good things were happening for the Presley family. When World War II ended in the summer of 1945, Vernon Presley's job in the war plant in Memphis ended. This meant he could come home to Tupelo.

Elvis Meets the Six-String

Accounts vary about when Elvis got his first guitar. Some say he received it as a gift for his ninth or tenth birthday. Another account says he got it the day after a small tornado hit Tupelo on January 7, 1946. We know that the guitar was purchased at a hardware store run by F. L. Bobo. Bobo recalled that when Elvis and his mother came in that day Elvis wanted to buy a rifle but didn't have enough money. Gladys wanted him to buy a guitar instead. According to Bobo, she told Elvis that she would make up the difference for him to buy a guitar, but not a rifle.[6]

According to another account, Elvis wanted a bicycle instead of the guitar. Again, Gladys tried to help Elvis make his decision. "Son, wouldn't you rather have the guitar?" Gladys reportedly said. "It would help you with your singing, and everyone does enjoy hearing you sing."[7]

In the end, Elvis decided to get the guitar. According to Bobo, it cost $7.75.[8]

Several people helped Elvis learn to play his new instrument. Two uncles taught him some chords. But it was the new pastor, young Frank Smith, who really helped Elvis learn to play.

As his skill and confidence grew, Elvis began playing at church. At first, he was shy. Smith had to call on him to perform. "I would have to insist on him [getting up there], he didn't push himself," Smith recalled. "He sang

In middle school and high school, Elvis honed his showmanship. He frequently brought his guitar to school to play for his friends and later entered and won a school talent show.

quite a few times, and he was liked."[9] Elvis also taught himself to play the piano.

In seventh grade, Elvis began taking his guitar to school almost every day. Often he would play and sing in the school basement, which served as a recess area. "He'd bring his guitar swung over his back and put it in his locker till lunchtime," his friend James Ausborn later recalled. "Then everybody would set around, and he would sing and strum on that guitar. All he talked about was music—not the Opry so much as gospel music. That was what he sung mostly."[10]

The guitar did not make Elvis particularly popular, however. Most of his classmates described him as shy or a loner. Others made fun of him for playing "hillbilly" music. Still, Elvis continued to sing. He often told classmates that someday he would sing at the Grand Ole Opry.[11]

On his last day at school, Elvis gave a little concert for his classmates. The last song he sang was "A Leaf on a Tree." Classmate Leroy Green later claimed that he went up to Elvis at the end and said, "Elvis, one of these days you're gonna be famous." Little did he know just how prophetic those words would be.[12]

3
A New Life in Memphis

Everything the family owned fit "on the top and in the trunk of a 1939 Plymouth," Elvis later recalled.[1] In November 1948, the Presley family took that car and headed north to Memphis, in search of a better life. They certainly found it, but not immediately.

Off to High School

The Presleys moved into the Lauderdale Courts public housing project in September 1949, just as Elvis was starting high school. To the Presleys, the apartment marked a huge step forward in their standard of living. They went from living in a single room to having two bedrooms, a living room, a kitchen, and a bathroom they did not have to share with another family.

Both Gladys and Vernon wanted Elvis to have a full high-school education. In those days, many working-class children dropped out when they were fifteen or sixteen to get full-time jobs. The Presleys, however, believed a high-school diploma was the key to a better life.

During his first two years at Humes High, Elvis melted into the crowd. He earned mostly average grades—Bs in many subjects with a smattering of As. In eighth grade, he earned one interesting C—in music. He claimed that the teacher, Miss Marmann, simply did not appreciate his type of singing.[2]

Teachers found him shy and polite. "He was a gentle, obedient boy, and he always went out of his way to try to do what you asked him to do," said Susie Johnson, his ninth-grade homeroom teacher.[3]

Over time, Elvis began to feel more at home in Memphis. He and his friends played football, rode bikes, and hung out at the local public pool during warm weather. Sometimes they ventured onto Beale Street, which was home to many well-known clubs featuring blues music.

Creating His Own Style

Elvis soon found himself drawn to the type of clothes that blues musicians wore. He bought some of these clothes used in thrift shops. Other items came from Lansky Brothers, a clothing store that catered to musicians. He remained a regular customer there for life.

At a time when most kids dressed in jeans and simple shirts, Elvis often wore black pants and pink shirts. He let his hair grow long and groomed it with hair tonic and Vaseline until it was slick and stiff. He grew sideburns as well. He certainly stood out in the crowd.

One year, Elvis decided to try out for the football team. The coach told him that he would have to cut his hair first. In the end, Elvis decided it wasn't worth it.

Another time, a bunch of guys cornered Elvis and threatened to cut his hair. A boy named Bobby "Red" West stepped in to stop them. Red was a big kid—a football player. The other kids backed down. Red became a lifelong friend to Elvis. In fact, Red later became a sometime bodyguard for many years.

Earning Money and Chipping In

Throughout his high-school years, Elvis held a variety of part-time jobs. He gave some of the money to his parents

"MOST TALENTED"?

Most high school yearbooks have sections devoted to listing the people from the senior class who classmates believe are "Most Popular," "Most Talented," or "Most Likely to Succeed." Elvis Presley, who went on to become one of the world's most famous people, earned none of those titles at Humes High. Still, the senior class prophecy did include a hint of things to come. It said, "We are reminded at this time to not forget to invite you all out to the 'Silver Horse' on Onion [sic] Ave. to hear the singing hillbillies of the road. Elvis Presley, Albert Teague, Doris Wilburn, and Mary Ann Propst are doing a bit of picking and singing out that away."

Oddly enough, Elvis was not voted "most talented" in his class. The graduate who would later become one of the most world's most famous people drew very little notice among his classmates.

Growing up in the years after the Great Depression, Elvis had to work through high school to help his parents make ends meet, often falling asleep in class because of his long work hours.

to help make ends meet. The rest he kept for clothes and dates.

Despite Elvis chipping in, the Presley family struggled financially. Chronic back problems prevented Vernon from doing many of the manual labor jobs for which he was best suited. Gladys worked a variety of jobs. The one she liked best was working as a nurses' aide at nearby St. Joseph Hospital.

Meanwhile, Gladys suffered with her own health problems. She felt frustrated at the family's lack of financial security. Often, she and Vernon argued about money. To forget about her problems, she turned to alcohol.

Sometimes she took diet pills as well. The combination took a toll on her health.

At one point when both Vernon and Gladys were unemployed, Elvis began working a full-shift job from 3:00 to 11:00 p.m. in addition to attending school. Soon, however, he began falling asleep in class, and his grades plummeted. Finally, he quit the job to focus on school.

For a while, the Presleys went on welfare, much to Gladys's shame. Then at another point when both Gladys and Vernon had relatively stable jobs, they earned too much to live in the projects. On January 7, 1953, just before Elvis's eighteenth birthday, they moved out of the projects forever.

A LADIES' MAN

Elvis maintained his interest in girls while in high school. His first real crush was on a girl named Sue. She worked at the candy counter of the movie theater where Elvis worked as an usher, and she gave him free candy. He ended up getting fired for punching another usher who tattled on them.[4]

Elvis dated many girls in high school. He went to the senior prom with Regis Wilson Vaughn, the girl he was dating at the time. Still, he had not been really serious about any of the girls he dated throughout high school. Surely, however, the girls all would be very serious about Elvis later—when their first love became a bona fide rock star.

Making Music

Elvis maintained his interest in music throughout high school. Memphis was home to blues legend B. B. King and many other blues artists. You could also find many other styles of music there, including hillbilly and gospel.

Jesse Lee Denson, the son of a preacher, gave Elvis guitar lessons. Together with some other boys, they gave informal concerts on Market Mall, a path that ran through the middle of the Courts apartments.

Elvis also became a regular at a little record store called Charlie's. One time Elvis told Johnny Black, another musician who spent time at Charlie's, "Johnny, someday I'm going to be driving Cadillacs." Even then he aspired to greatness.[5]

At noon on Saturdays, Elvis went downtown to the WMPS radio studio for the *High Noon Round-Up* show. The nationally known Blackwood Brothers Quartet appeared live there.

James Blackwood, one of the group's founders, remembered Elvis from those days. So did Jack Hess, lead singer for a gospel group called the Statesmen, What made Elvis stand out from the hundreds of other fans? "He was just nice, a nice kid, this bright-eyed boy asking all kinds of questions, and asking in a way that you would really want to tell him," Hess said.[6]

In high school, Elvis participated in the senior class variety show. Approximately thirty acts took part. The performer who received the most applause would be the winner of the competition. Elvis won easily. Observers said that many in the audience cried during his performance. It is said that one girl even fainted.

On June 3, 1953, Elvis received his diploma from Humes High School. He was the first member of his immediate family to earn a diploma. He displayed it proudly for many years. As he looked forward to life beyond high school, he dreamed of a career in music. But he had no idea how he would get there.

4

Starting on the Road to Success

Elvis Presley's road to music success took a detour through some other jobs first. Soon after high school, he went to work at Precision Tool Company. He hated the work, but he was proud to help support the family.

In January 1954, Elvis became a truck driver for Crown Electric. He enjoyed being outside, and he earned forty-five dollars a week. That was good money in 1954. A gallon of milk cost ninety-two cents that year, and a gallon of gas cost twenty-one cents.[1]

Elvis gave most of the money he earned to his parents. He carried his guitar with him in the truck many days. Mrs. Gladys Tipler, who owned the company with her husband, sometimes teased him about it. "Elvis, put down that gi-tar," she said. "It's gonna be the ruination of you. You better make up your mind what you're gonna do."[2]

Into the Studio

In many ways, he already knew what he was going to do. In 1953 he went to Memphis Recording Service, which later became known as Sun Studio. There he paid about four dollars to record "My Happiness" and "That's When Your Heartaches Begin." At the end of his session, office

Sun Studio, in Memphis, Tennessee, was the first professional home of Elvis Presley. For the price of four dollars, he was able to record his first songs in 1953.

manager Marion Keisker made this note: "Good ballad singer. Hold."[3]

Owner Sam Phillips had told her that he was searching for a white man who had the sound and feel of a black musician. Keisker thought she might have found the right person in Elvis.

Still, nothing came of that contact for some time. Elvis met Phillips when he returned to the studio in January 1954. This time he recorded two country songs, "I'll Never Stand in Your Way" and "It Wouldn't Be the Same Without You." Phillips still had no assignment for him, and Elvis began to wonder if he would ever get his "break."

His First Break

That summer, Elvis got his first big break. Phillips was looking for a singer to record a song titled "Without You." He couldn't even remember Elvis's name. He asked for the "kid with the sideburns." According to Keisker, when she called, Elvis literally ran all the way to the studio arriving out of breath while she was still holding the phone.[4]

Elvis did not feel that he captured any magic with the song, and it was never released. However, Phillips was impressed enough to invite Elvis to continue singing. For the next couple of hours, he sang a little bit of everything—blues, gospel, and country.

Phillips believed that Elvis could succeed with the proper backing. Soon after, he brought Elvis into the studio to rehearse with talented bass player Bill Black and guitarist Scotty Moore.

On July 5, 1954, Elvis recorded "That's All Right," his version of a song recorded by noted blues artist Arthur

A STEADY GIRL

In January 1954, nineteen-year-old Elvis began attending the Assembly of God Church in Memphis. It was through the church that Elvis first saw fourteen-year-old Dixie Locke, who found herself strangely attracted to the shy young man with the greasy black hair and colorful clothes. She introduced herself to him at a Sunday evening event at the Rainbow Rollerdrome. The two immediately hit it off.

Elvis described Dixie this way: "She was kind of small with long, dark hair that came down to her shoulders and the biggest smile I've ever seen anywhere. She was always laughing, always enjoying herself. . . . For two years we had a ball."[5]

Often, Elvis and Dixie would go to Riverside Park, which was full of young couples. Many times, Elvis would get out his guitar and sing. "People were just mesmerized, and he loved being the center of attention," Dixie recalled.[6]

Crudup in the 1940s. Everyone could sense the magic in this upbeat number, which seemed a cross between country music and blues music. It became Elvis's first hit.

On July 8, the song made its debut on the local "Red Hot and Blue" show on radio Station WHBQ.

Due to the heavy volume of requests, the disc jockey played the record an amazing fourteen times in a row. Soon "That's All Right" rose to number three on the Memphis country-and-western chart.[7]

Elvis signed with Sun Records owner Sam Phillips in 1954, and he would go on to become Sun's biggest star, with only Johnny Cash coming close to his level of popularity.

Later that month, Elvis signed a contract with Sun Records. Because he was under twenty-one years of age, his parents had to sign it as well. The two-year contract called for a minimum of eight record sides over a period of two years. The royalty rate was three percent of the wholesale price.

Later in July, Elvis performed his first concert. He served as the opening act for well-known country singer Slim Whitman at the Overton Park Shell in Memphis. Elvis later said that he was so nervous onstage that his legs began to shake. Thus began the leg shake that would become his trademark.[8]

As Elvis sang that day, the crowd hooted. He thought they were making fun of him, and he slunk offstage after singing "Blue Moon of Kentucky."

But his friends backstage were elated. They realized the crowd's noises meant they were excited by the music. His friends pushed him back onstage for an encore. "The girls love you," they told him. "It's the way you shake."[9]

In early August, *Billboard* published a review in its "Spotlight" section. Editor Paul Ackerman called Elvis "A potent new chanter who can sock over a tune for either the country or the r & b [rhythm and blues] markets. . . . A strong new talent."[10] *Billboard* was a respected music magazine. Its endorsement helped set the stage for Elvis's wider popularity.

Soon, things started happening in a blur. Offers to perform continued to pile up. Elvis, Scotty, and Bill began playing each weekend in the Eagle's Nest, a popular nightclub in Memphis. Then on October 2, they got to play at the world famous Grand Ole Opry in Nashville, Tennessee. To be invited there was a great tribute to a singer and band that had been together just a few months and had just two songs to their credit.

According to some reports, Elvis earned polite, but unenthusiastic, applause. Others said the performance was a disaster. One popular story circulated over the years is that Jim Denny, the director of the Grand Ole Opry, told Elvis that he ought to stick to driving a truck. Other historians report that Denny said Elvis was "not bad" but not right for the Grand Ole Opry.[11]

Meanwhile, Elvis, Scotty, and Bill landed a spot on the *Louisiana Hayride*. This weekly show in Shreveport, Louisiana, helped launch the careers of many country stars. During their first performance, the audience did

SUN STUDIO

Sun Studio, where Elvis made some of his first recordings, is today a small museum on Union Street in Memphis. While not nearly the same tourist draw as Elvis's estate at Graceland, it does attract many people who want to see where Elvis got his start as a recording artist. Many other famous singers also recorded there, including Johnny Cash, Roy Orbison, Charlie Rich, Jerry Lee Lewis and others. The building has been designated as a U.S. National Historic Landmark. The museum houses lots of memorabilia from the recording studio's early days.

not quite know what to make of Elvis and his band. Elvis sounded different from anyone they had ever heard before. However, the teenagers in the audience soon were captivated by his look and his music.

Elvis and his band soon earned an invitation to play every Saturday night for a year. Every weekend the band made the seven-hour drive from Memphis to Shreveport. Elvis received $18 per show, while Scotty and Bill earned $12 apiece.

Around this time, Elvis quit his job as a truck driver. Singing had become a full-time job. Elvis soon became the most popular performer at the *Louisiana Hayride*. Therefore, his act always closed the show. At his last performance ever at the *Louisiana Hayride* the announcer stated, "Elvis has left the building" as a way to calm down the crowd. In the 1970s, "Elvis has left the building" became a fairly standard line for closing his shows.

In late December 1954, Elvis signed a management contract with Bob Neal, a disc jockey at WMPS in Memphis. Before year's end, he released another record titled "Milkcow Blues Boogie/You're a Heartbreaker." He also bought a tan 1951 Lincoln for the group to do its traveling. On the side was painted the words: "Elvis Presley—Sun Records."[12]

Elvis bought himself a 1942 Martin guitar. It cost him $175, which was a great deal of money in those days. The man at the store bought his used guitar for eight dollars and promptly threw it in the trash.[13]

In just a few short months, Elvis had gone from an unknown singer to a fast-rising star. But his success in 1954 was nothing compared to what lay ahead in 1955. Elvis mania would soon sweep the United States and beyond.

5

Becoming the King

Elvis Presley had many reasons to be excited as 1955 began. On January 5, he topped the bill at the City Auditorium in San Angelo, Texas, although they misspelled his name as "Alvis Presley." At the end of the show, hundreds of teenaged girls rushed the stage seeking autographs.[1] Elvis and his band continued on a whirlwind tour for the rest of January through Texas, Arkansas, Louisiana, and Mississippi.

It soon became clear that Elvis drew most of the fans to the shows. To this point, Elvis had been receiving fifty percent of the money. Manager Bob Neal proposed that instead of getting a percentage, Scotty and Bill should receive a salary. Needless to say, they did not appreciate the change. They threatened to quit but then agreed to stay.

A New Manager

It was clear that Elvis was becoming a bigger and bigger star. But he still felt frustrated. He wanted to break through on a national level. Then Colonel Tom Parker took over the management of Elvis's career in the 1950s.

Parker helped country star Eddy Arnold reach the top of the country charts. But the two got into an argument,

GIRLS, GIRLS, GIRLS!

Elvis's popularity soon grew to the point where he found himself in danger. Girls swooned at his hip-swinging performances. Meanwhile, their boyfriends boiled with jealousy. After a performance in Lubbock, Texas, a man in a car called Elvis to come over. The man punched Elvis in the face and sped off.

During a show at the Gator Bowl football stadium in Florida in May 1955, Elvis joked that he'd see the girls in the audience backstage after the show. A gate had been left open, and girls poured into the backstage area. They literally ripped most of the clothes off his body in their frenzy.

and Arnold fired him, so Parker sought a new performer he could make into a star. When he heard about Elvis, he was intrigued. He began attending some of his concerts. He realized that Elvis's popularity could generate the kind of riots that singer Frank Sinatra had inspired in the 1940s. "And from then on, when he went to Elvis's shows, it was the crowd Parker watched, not Elvis," wrote biographer Alanna Nash.[2]

In February 1955, Parker met with Sam Phillips and Neal. He told Phillips that Elvis could not succeed on a small-time label such as Sun. Needless to say, Phillips was

Fans loved Elvis. At the New York premiere of his first film, *Love Me Tender*, girls went wild, screaming and crying when the King of Rock and Roll appeared on the silver screen.

not happy at the thought of losing his biggest recording star. He rebuffed Parker's offer.

Meanwhile, despite all the touring, Elvis, Scotty, and Bill took time to record some new songs. One of these songs, "Baby Let's Play House" became the next single.

Amid all the success, Elvis did have one disappointment. He auditioned for Arthur Godfrey's *Talent Scouts* in New York. He hoped exposure on the popular television show could help take his music nationwide. The audition did not go well, and they never even got to meet Godfrey.

Breaking Up

Still, Elvis and his band kept touring nearly nonstop throughout the spring and summer. On May 6, Elvis returned to Memphis to attend Dixie Locke's junior prom. Soon after, however, they broke up. The rigors of his touring life tore them apart.

Indeed both Dixie and Gladys Presley sensed that the man they both loved was slipping away from them. "It grew hard for her to let everybody have him," Dixie said. "I had the same feelings. He did not belong to [us] anymore."[3]

"RECORD" POPULARITY

In 1956 and 1957, Elvis Presley dominated the music charts as no other recording artist had ever done before. It seemed as though the amazing run of chart-topping songs he had might never be broken. Then came the Beatles. This British group rode a tidal wave of popularity that has yet to be equaled. On April 4, 1964, the Beatles held all top five spots on *Billboard Magazine*'s Hot 100 chart of the most popular songs in the United States. "Can't Buy Me Love" was number 1, followed by "Twist and Shout," "She Loves You," "I Want to Hold Your Hand," and "Please Please Me." The Beatles credited Elvis with being one of their early influences when they were getting started.

A Nationwide Hit

In July 1955, "Baby, Let's Play House" became Elvis's first record to make the nationwide country music charts. These charts reflect the popularity of songs across

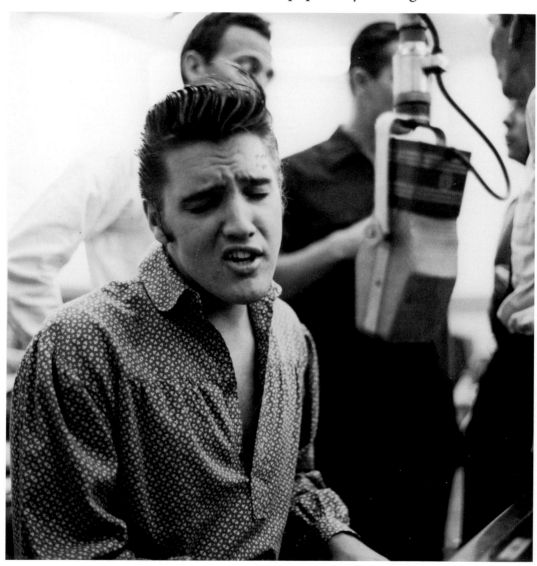

In 1955, Elvis left Sun Records for the larger RCA, where his new manager, Colonel Tom Parker, believed he could become a much bigger star.

America. Also that month, Elvis got a new Martin D-28 guitar. It came with a tooled leather cover that prevented the back of the instrument from getting scratched by Elvis's belt buckle when he performed.

Elvis and the band recorded three new songs in July: "I Forgot to Remember to Forget," "Mystery Train," and "Trying to Get to You." "Mystery Train" became his next single release.

Meanwhile, several things were happening that would propel Elvis's career to the next level. Colonel Tom Parker was named a "special advisor" to help promote the singer. He proved to be a master of promotion.

Late in 1955, Parker convinced RCA to pay Phillips $35,000 to bring Elvis from Sun Records to RCA. Elvis also received a $5,000 signing bonus. Today, that seems like a ridiculously low price to buy the contract for the person who would turn out to be arguably the biggest star in the history of popular music. In 1955, however, that figure was "more than had ever been paid before to buy out a performer's contract.[4]

RCA was taking a risk based on Elvis's potential. At the time, he had very little national recognition. RCA's risk soon paid off in spectacular fashion.

Meanwhile, Phillips was sorry to lose the star attraction from his record label. However, the cash he received for his star's contract would allow him to work with more artists and help launch other careers.

Phillips summed up his feelings this way: "I feel Elvis is one of the most talented youngsters today, and by releasing his contract to RCA-Victor we will give him the opportunity of entering the largest organization of its kind in the world, so his talents can be given the fullest opportunity."[5]

A week later, Elvis sent a thank-you telegram to Parker. In it he said, "I've always known and now my folks are assured that you are the best, most wonderful person I could ever hope to work with. Believe me when I say I will stick with you through thick and thin and do everything I can to uphold your faith in me."[6]

Parker kept pushing on behalf of his client. He contacted the William Morris talent agency about having Elvis star in a movie. He likened Elvis to movie star James Dean, who had recently died in an automobile accident. "If you ever follow one of my hunches, follow up on this one and you won't go wrong," Parker said.[7]

Meanwhile, Parker worked to establish exclusive control over Elvis's career.

Because Elvis was only twenty, both of his parents would have to approve and sign any contracts. Vernon agreed right away. Gladys held out. Eventually, Parker won Gladys over—at least enough to get her signature. When Neal's contract expired in March 1956, Parker took over as Elvis's exclusive manager, a position he held for the rest of the singer's life. For his efforts, Parker at first received twenty-five percent of Elvis's total earnings.

Best Year Ever

Under Parker's shrewd guidance, and using his own great talent, Elvis set out to hit the top. And the year he had in 1956 ranks among the most successful year ever for a recording artist.

On January 10, 1956, Elvis recorded his first song for RCA-Victor. And what a song it was. "Heartbreak Hotel" topped the national popular music charts for an amazing eight weeks beginning in April. The song made Elvis a national sensation and moved him from being a country star to being a rock-and-roll star.

With depressing lyrics and unique guitar and piano riffs, "Heartbreak Hotel" was unlike other popular songs of the time. Elvis managed to capture its raw emotion perfectly. On January 28, Elvis appeared on *Stage Show*, a national television show. The theater in New York City where the show was filmed was not nearly filled. Elvis may have been a star in the South, but the people in New York City did not know him yet. They did after this performance, as did people throughout America.

Elvis jerked and twisted as he sang. According to biographer Jerry Hopkins, "He sneered, dropped his eyelids, and smiled out of the left side of his mouth.

BANNED RECORDS

By today's standards, Elvis Presley's records and his performances seem tame. Yet after one concert in Los Angeles in 1957, the police showed up and warned his manager that unless the next night's show was toned down, Elvis might go to jail. That same year, a number of U.S. radio stations banned his Christmas album because they didn't believe a rock and roll artist should be singing religious songs. Elvis is hardly alone in having his music banned or lyrics censored. Other artists ranging from the Beatles and Rolling Stones to Adele and Lady Gaga have had songs censored or banned. Reasons include references to drugs, sexual suggestiveness, and use of profanity.

He used every physical trick that had come to him in the 16 months since his first record was released."[8]

Soon Elvis also appeared on Milton Berle's popular television show. Ratings skyrocketed, but not everyone was impressed. Ben Gross of the *New York Daily News* wrote that "Elvis's grunt and groin antics were suggestive and vulgar."[9]

His gyrations earned him the nickname "Elvis the Pelvis." He found that offensive. "My pelvis has nothing to do with what I do," he said.[10]

Parker loved the controversy. All the attention made Elvis's records sell even faster. In all, Elvis released four chart-topping songs in 1956. In addition to "Heartbreak Hotel," the others were "I Want You, I Need You, I Love You," "Don't Be Cruel/Hound Dog," and "Love Me Tender." "Love Me Tender" remains one of Elvis's most popular ballads even today.

It was a remarkable run. No other artist would enjoy that type of success until nearly a decade later, when the Beatles held down the top five spots all at once during one magic week in April 1964.

Not only were Elvis's records hot, but so were his television performances. Throughout 1956, he appeared on many television shows, including two performances on the wildly popular *Ed Sullivan Show*. He made a third appearance in early 1957. The performances drew huge television audiences and cemented Elvis's stature as an American icon.

Elvis used his newfound riches to support his family. In 1955, he had moved his parents into a rented house in Memphis. In March 1956, he bought a house in one of the nicest areas of Memphis. He paid forty thousand dollars in cash, a huge sum in those days.

Elvis was pleased to be able to make life better for his parents—especially his beloved Gladys.

But as Elvis's fame continued to grow, the Presleys struggled to enjoy their new home. Fans, mostly young women, rang the doorbell at all hours of the day and night hoping to catch a glimpse of their hero. Sometimes crowds of girls hung out on the sidewalk outside waiting for Elvis to enter or to exit the house.

Elvis spent money freely. April 1956, he owned forty suits and twenty-seven pairs of shoes.[11] He also bought Gladys a pink Cadillac, even though she didn't like to drive.

When Elvis started making real money as a singer, one of the first things he did was help his parents live a more comfortable life— including buying them a new home in Memphis.

Still, even with his growing fame and money Elvis often found himself unhappy. Now that he was on top, he felt the pressure to stay there. Further, everywhere he went, crowds followed. This loss of privacy bothered him.

Elvis also struggled to have a meaningful relationship with women, although he continued to sleep with women in many of the towns he visited. During 1955 and 1956, he was linked with several women, including actress Natalie Wood.

Elvis spent the most time with June Juanico. In many ways, they seemed perfectly matched. She said that he proposed to her in the summer of 1956, with the agreement that they would wait a few years until his career was solidly established. In the end, she decided not to wait for him. She married another man in 1957.

Elvis also had to worry that overeager fans might hurt him in their enthusiasm. As the crowds grew larger and rowdier, Elvis hired Red West, a big burly young man he had met in high school to be his bodyguard.

Lights! Camera! Action!

As his records continued to climb the charts and his concerts continued to sell out, Elvis also undertook a new challenge. In late March 1956, Parker arranged for Elvis to do a movie screen test for famed producer Hal Wallis at Paramount Studios in Hollywood. In early April, Wallis offered a contract for one motion picture with options to make six more.

Shooting began in August for *The Reno Brothers*, the story about three Confederate soldiers who were unaware the Civil War had ended. Elvis played Clint Reno. One of the songs he recorded for the movie, "Love Me Tender," seemed destined to be a hit. To capitalize on that, the name of the movie was changed to *Love Me Tender*. The title song went to number one on the music charts.

In September, Elvis returned to Tupelo, Mississippi, to perform a special homecoming concert for five thousand screaming fans. Another highlight came in December when Elvis joined Jerry Lee Lewis and Carl Perkins for a late-night jam session at Sun Studios. Johnny Cash also dropped by. The impromptu session became known as the Million Dollar Quartet. All four were later inducted into the Rock and Roll Hall of Fame.

The music, the movies, the image. It was all part of Parker's strategy to build Elvis into the biggest star the world had ever known. Parker even turned Elvis into a brand name, licensing seventy-eight different products, ranging from Elvis charm bracelets to glow-in-the-dark busts over the years. In 1956 alone, sales of Elvis-related items totaled $22 million.[12]

"No artist had ever exploded on the scene with the volcanic impact of Elvis Presley in 1956, and no manager before Tom Parker had ever been so brilliantly, or blatantly, capitalistic," wrote Elvis biographer Nash. "At a time when most managers did little more for their artists than book concert dates, Parker perpetually figured out new ways to exploit his star."[13]

The strategy paid off. In October 1956, *Variety* magazine dubbed Elvis "the King of Rock 'n' Roll"—a nickname that would stick with him throughout his life.[14]

As 1956 ended, Elvis stood atop the world. What would come next?

6

On His Throne

I t seemed impossible that Elvis Presley could maintain the momentum of the biggest year in music history. Amazingly, he followed with another year that was just as big. Once again he charted four number-one hits: "Too Much," "All Shook Up," "(Let Me Be Your) Teddy Bear," and "Jailhouse Rock/Treat Me Nice." Together, those records spent an amazing twenty-five weeks atop the charts—almost half the year.

Elvis also made two popular movies in 1957. In *Loving You*, he played a fame-bound hillbilly singer. According to writer/director Hal Kanter, "*Loving You* was probably a more realistic view of the Elvis persona, his life and his style, than any film that he made after that."[1]

Elvis's performance won over some critics of his acting. Jim Powers of the *Hollywood Reporter* said, "Presley . . . acts naturally and with appeal."[2]

In *Jailhouse Rock*, Elvis played an ex-convict who becomes a rock star. Despite mixed reviews, the film peaked at number three on the movie charts. The hard-driving song "Jailhouse Rock" did even better, spending seven weeks atop the music charts. Elvis helped choreograph the song-and-dance number that opens the film. It is probably the most famous scene from any of his movies. "Many modern-day music critics cite the sequence as the blueprint and inspiration for the music video genre," wrote Adam Victor.[3]

Amazing Graceland

Probably the biggest highlight of the year for the King of Rock and Roll was finding his castle. Eager to find a more secluded home where they could escape the legions of fans, Vernon and Gladys Presley found a mansion on the outskirts of Memphis that seemed suitable. Named Graceland, the house was set in a grove of oak trees.

On March 25, 1957, the Presleys purchased Graceland at a cost of $102,500. That figure represented a small fortune for a house in those days. The average annual wage in the United States in 1957 was $3,641.72.[4]

SINGER TURNED ACTOR

Throughout the 1960s, Elvis made a series of movies. Critics panned most of them. Some music historians believed that the time and effort Elvis spent making these movies took away from his music. Although Elvis was not the first singer to become an actor, his model set a trend that has lasted until the present. Other famous singers turned actors include Madonna, Michael Jackson, Cher, Snoop Dogg, Dolly Parton, Beyoncé, Jennifer Hudson, Justin Timberlake, and Mark Wahlberg. Some have earned critical acclaim for their acting. Others, like Elvis, endured criticism.

While Elvis's music was a big part of his mass appeal, his film appearances drove fans crazy. One of his biggest hits of the era was the musical prison romp _Jailhouse Rock_.

For a while, Gladys enjoyed decorating the family's new home. Soon, however, she felt as caged at Graceland as she had in their previous home. Fans hung around outside the estate's fence at all hours of the day and night, hoping for a glimpse of Elvis. She soon told a friend, "I can't go buy my own groceries. I can't go to the movies. I can't see my neighbors. I'm the most miserable woman in the world."[5]

Right after buying Graceland, Elvis returned to the road. Then he headed back to Hollywood to film _Jailhouse Rock_. Although he never formally studied acting, he carefully reviewed his performance each day and looked for ways to make it better. "I always criticize myself in films," he told one interviewer. "I'm always striving to be natural in front of a camera. That takes studying, of a sort."[6]

In *Jailhouse Rock*, Elvis's character killed someone. Over the course of the movie he serves time in prison and then becomes a rock star when he is released.

Though Graceland was primarily home to Elvis's parents when he first bought the property outside Memphis, Tennessee, fans swarmed to the house hoping to catch sight of the King.

Record companies and Hollywood welcome him with open arms. Meanwhile, Elvis, who was really pretty clean-cut, found his records banned in many places.

An essayist in the *Catholic Sun* called Elvis's music a "voodoo of frustration and defiance." And the *New York Daily News* described rock and roll in general as "a barrage of primitive jungle-beat rhythm set to lyrics which few adults would care to hear."[7]

A True Star

In September, 12,000 people attended a special benefit show Elvis did in Tupelo. The money raised supported the planned Elvis Presley Youth Center. The concert was a triumph. However, when Elvis returned to Tupelo a few years later he found that the center had not been built. No one knows what happened to the money that had been raised.

On October 28, Elvis performed for the first time in Hollywood. A sellout crowd went wild at his first show. Not everyone approved, however. The Los Angeles Vice Squad told Tom Parker that Elvis needed to tone down the show for the second night. Otherwise he might go to jail for indecency. The police actually showed up with movie cameras to film the second show. If Elvis did anything obscene, they would have proof on tape. The show that night was much tamer, however.

Even with all his success, all was not rosy for Elvis. Scotty Moore and Bill Black quit as his band members that fall. They felt they were not being paid enough. They each earned a hundred dollars a week at home and two hundred a week while on the road, but they had to pay all their own traveling expenses.

ROCK AND ROLL = REBELLION?

Why was rock and roll so disturbing to many adults? Before rock and roll, most popular music was quiet and mellow. Many songs featured piano music or acoustic guitars. Rock and roll was loud. It featured electric guitars and a driving drum beat. The lyrics sometimes seemed disrespectful of adults. Many parents feared that listening to rock and roll would lead their children into bad behavior and rebellion against authority. For that reason, many parents at first disliked rock and roll music and artists such as Elvis Presley. Over time, however, rock and roll simply became a part of popular culture.

The boys did come back and play on a day-by-day basis sometimes as needed, but it was never the same after that.

Meanwhile, Elvis's concerts still exuded raw power. They still drew hordes of screaming fans. But Elvis sensed something was missing—at least for him. "There was nothing new," wrote biographer Peter Guralnick. "For the first time in a long time he was no longer sure what was supposed to happen next."[8]

Elvis felt the same discomfort when he got back to Memphis. He told the Reverend James Hamill, "I am the most miserable young man you have ever seen. I have got more money than I can ever spend. I have thousands of

In 1958, Elvis Presley was sworn in to the United States Army along with hundreds of other young men who had been drafted to serve their country.

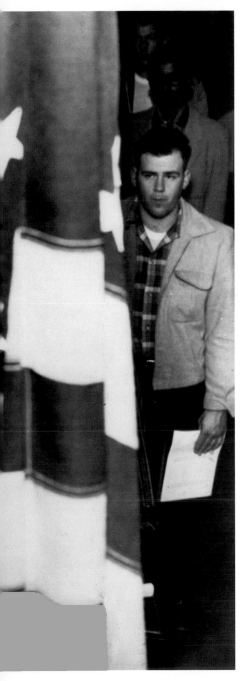

fans out there, and I have a lot of people who call themselves my friends, but I am miserable."[9]

Actually, Elvis had more than thousands of fans. He had millions. Many of them organized fan clubs for their hero. Marion Keisker of Sun Records set up the first one just weeks after Elvis recorded his first single. As his fame spread, similar clubs formed across the world. By 1956, Elvis received an astounding ten thousand letters a week.

Meanwhile, Gladys's health continued to decline. Even after the move to Graceland, she felt the lack of privacy. She could not go out in public without being noticed. Furthermore, she worried about Elvis whenever he traveled.

To forget her troubles, Gladys turned to liquor. She also took diet pills. Together, the two took a heavy toll on her health. "From about July [1957] on, Gladys just seemed to lose interest in everything," recalled Lillian.[10]

Drafted!

All of Elvis's success could not prevent him from facing the same fate as thousands of other young people across the United States—being drafted. At the time, there were not enough volunteers to fill the needed slots in the U.S. armed services. Therefore, young men registered for the draft when they turned eighteen and went into the service if and when their name was drawn by the draft board.

In mid-December 1957, the Memphis Draft Board let it be known that Elvis would soon receive his draft notice. Almost immediately, the army, navy, and air force contacted him. If he volunteered before he was drafted, he could pick his branch of the service. Each offered him a special deal.

For instance, the army offered Elvis a role in its Special Services branch. There he would travel around and entertain the troops. Manager Parker refused to even consider it. "If they want my boy to sing," he said, "they are going to have to pay for it like anyone else."[11]

Instead, Elvis was drafted into the army as a regular soldier. The two-year commitment threatened his wildly successful career. Fans are fickle. During the two years Elvis would be away, his fans might transfer their allegiance to other singers.

Still, Parker thought army service would transform Presley's image and make him an even bigger star. Elvis "would look like a hero," noted Parker biographer Alanna Nash.[12]

Elvis took the news of his impending army service well. Talking to reporters, Elvis said, "I'm kind-a proud of it. It's a duty I've got to fill and I'm gonna do it."[13]

Parker insisted to Elvis that he should be treated like everyone else in the army. Elvis agreed. He did ask for one accommodation, though. He asked the draft board for a deferment—or postponement—in the date of his induction so that he could shoot his next movie, *King Creole*. He was not asking for himself, he noted, but on behalf of Paramount, "so these folks will not lose so much money, with everything they have done so far."[14] The draft board agreed that Elvis would be inducted on March 20 rather than in January.

Elvis returned to Hollywood in January to film *King Creole*. By this time, he traveled with an entourage of nearly a dozen friends. They helped with various things, from driving his car to serving as his bodyguard. The innermost members of this group became known as the Memphis Mafia.

King Creole tells the story of a singer who works as a busboy in a bar called King Creole on Bourbon Street in New Orleans. It remained Elvis's personal favorite of all the films he was to make.

The movie also drew favorable reviews. The *New York Times* simply ran a headline that said, "Elvis can act!"

After the movie was finished filming, Elvis had just ten days to spend at Graceland before entering the army. He he wondered if his career would still be alive when he finished.

7

Serving His Country

Elvis's induction into the US Army on March 24, 1958, became a media circus. When he arrived at his local draft board at 6:35 a.m., a horde of reporters and photographers were waiting for him.

That afternoon, Elvis and a dozen other recruits boarded a bus bound for Fort Chaffee, Arkansas. The next day, fifty-five reporters and photographers watched as Elvis received the traditional army crew cut. Elvis caught some of the falling hair, and quipped, "Hair today, gone tomorrow."[1] Asked about his new barracks buddies, Elvis responded, "They've been swell to me. They treat me like anyone else, though. That's the way I want it."[2]

Next, Elvis reported to Fort Hood, Texas. There he completed eight weeks of basic training, followed by fourteen weeks of more specialized training. He settled into army life fairly easily. He didn't mind rising early. "There's not much difference between this and making a movie," he said. "In Hollywood, you have to get up at 5 A.M. and be on the set at 6."[3]

Officers and other soldiers alike admired Elvis's positive attitude and work ethic. His fans vowed not to forget him while he was in the army. In fact, he received fifteen thousand letters a week while he was at Fort Hood.

All of the letters were forwarded to Parker's office in Madison, Tennessee.

Losing His Mother

Probably the biggest adjustment for Elvis was being out of touch with his mother. Even when he toured, he called home often. During basic training, he could not. In this era before cell phones, there were few phones on base. Most were restricted for official army use only. Finally, after two

Although Elvis was already a bona fide star, he took his role in the army seriously, and his fellow soldiers admired him for his positive attitude and strong work ethic.

weeks Elvis had a chance to call his mother. For the next hour, recalled his friend Eddie Fadal, "they were crying and moaning on the telephone—hardly a word was spoken."[4]

Elvis received a furlough to visit home in late May and early June. While home, Elvis attended a preview of his new movie, *King Creole*. He also traveled to Nashville for a recording session—his last for the next two years. From that session came future hits, including "A Big Hunk o' Love," "A Fool Such as I," and "I Need Your Love Tonight." Those songs kept Elvis's music on the charts while he was in the army.

Soldiers who had family nearby were allowed to move out of the barracks. Therefore, when Elvis returned to Fort Hood, he rented a three-bedroom trailer home. Then Gladys and Vernon Presley joined him, along with Vernon's mother, Minnie, and Elvis's friend Lamar Fike. Later they moved to a house where they had more room.

While in Texas, Gladys's condition continued to decline. Years of drinking and taking diet pills had taken their toll on her body. In early August she went into the hospital back in Memphis. The doctors said she had hepatitis. This is an inflammation of the liver. Serious cases can be fatal.

Each day Gladys grew worse. On Tuesday, August 12, Elvis asked for emergency leave to go to her. He arrived in Memphis that evening. By this time, her condition was critical.

Elvis stayed at his mother's bedside for a full day. She died during the next night. Elvis was heartbroken. "He could not stop stroking her body and calling for her to come back," wrote Elvis biographer Marie Clayton.[5]

A FUNERAL AT GRACELAND

As the news of Gladys's death spread, a crowd gathered outside the gates at Graceland. The funeral became a public spectacle. It took sixty-five police cars to escort the procession of mourners to the cemetery.

Elvis had been extremely close to his mother. Her death hit him hard. He cried throughout much of the funeral. "Everything I have is gone," he wailed.[6]

But while Elvis mourned his mother, it's likely that most of the funeral spectators knew little about the woman the King so loved. It's highly probable that the majority of the spectators turned up solely to catch a glimpse of Elvis.

Elvis's Aunt Lillian believed he never fully recovered from his mother's death. After Gladys died, "[h]e changed completely," she said.[7]

Stationed Overseas

Still, life went on. Elvis returned to his army training in Texas. Soon he prepared to leave for West Germany. In the late 1950s, Germany was divided into two parts. East Germany had a communist government. It was backed by the Soviet Union. West Germany was a democracy. It was backed by the United States and its allies.

Elvis and his father, Vernon, on the front steps of Graceland on August 14, 1958, hours after the death of Elvis's mother, Gladys. For Elvis, who had been exceptionally close with his mother, the loss was especially difficult.

On September 22, 1958, Elvis climbed aboard the USS *General George M. Randall* as a military band played a medley of his rock-and-roll hits. He said that while he would be out of his fan's sight for awhile, "I hope I'm not out of their minds."[8]

Elvis arrived in West Germany on October 1. Swarms of fans greeted the ship, and he gave a press conference the following day. Then he was assigned his duty as a jeep driver on an army base in the town of Friedberg.

To help him feel less lonely, Elvis paid for his father and his grandmother Minnie to travel to Germany, along with his friends Red West and Lamar Fike. Given permission to move off base, Elvis and his group lived in a hotel for awhile. After they set a small fire while fooling around one day, the manager asked them to leave. Then they moved into the house of a woman named Frau Pieper in the town of Bad Nauheim. They stayed there the rest of Elvis's time in Germany.

Although Elvis was often asked to perform, he simply wanted to do his job as a soldier. "We've asked him and he said, 'I'd rather not, sir,'" said Major General Thomas F. Van Natta. "I think he feels he has an obligation to his country and he wants to pay it like everyone else and get it over with. . . . He's a good soldier."[9]

Indeed, by early 1960, Elvis had been promoted to the rank of sergeant. "Since his arrival, Presley has demonstrated leadership ability and proved himself worthy of promotion of sergeant," said Captain Hubert Childress, his company commander.[10]

While stationed in Germany, Elvis kept himself busy in many ways while off duty. For instance, he began to take up karate, which remained an interest throughout his life.

COLD COMFORT

It may have been while on maneuvers with his unit that Elvis began taking amphetamines, sometimes referred to as "speed." These are pills that help people keep awake and alert for long periods of time. They were also available as an appetite suppressant to help people lose weight. At the time, no prescription was needed to get amphetamines. Many soldiers took them, as did pilots, and long-haul truckers. However, for Elvis the pills posed special problems. He already had trouble sleeping. Taking pills that further disrupted his sleep patterns only made things worse.

Meanwhile, back home Elvis's records continued to sell well. Periodically, RCA would release some of the new songs Elvis had recorded before he left. At the same time, Parker negotiated new movie deals for Elvis. That way he could pick up his film career as soon as he returned from the army. Elvis also continued to earn money from his previous films. Indeed, Parker estimated that Elvis earned $2 million in 1958. This was an amazing amount in those days, especially considering that Elvis had spent most of the year in the service.[11]

Falling in Love

Elvis had many girlfriends while in Germany, including Vera Tschechowa, a beautiful eighteen-year-old German starlet. Meanwhile, he also kept in touch from time to time with Anita Wood, his girlfriend back home.

However, Elvis's most intriguing romance was with dark-haired beauty Priscilla Ann Beaulieu, the stepdaughter of US Air Force Captain Joseph Paul Beaulieu. She and Elvis were introduced through an airman named Currie Grant.

Twenty-four-year-old Elvis and felt an immediate attraction to Priscilla and the pair started spending time together. However, Priscilla was only fourteen years old, and she lived about an hour away. On their fourth date, her stepfather insisted on meeting Elvis. He grilled Elvis about his intentions. Elvis turned on the charm. Noting that Priscilla was very mature for her age, he talked about how lonely he was stationed so far from home. "I guess you might say I need someone to talk to," Elvis said. "You don't need to worry about her, Captain. I'll take good care of her."[12]

Captain Beaulieu allowed the two to date if they had a chaperone. Soon she was spending more and more evenings at Elvis's house. She understood that Elvis saw other women, but she accepted that.

Despite the special place she held in Elvis's heart, Priscilla worried about the many other girls who wanted him. Still, his relationship with Priscilla lasted throughout his stay in Germany.

Elvis felt safe talking with Priscilla about his innermost thoughts. "I really felt I got to know who Elvis Presley was during this time," she later said. "He was his most vulnerable, his most honest, I would say his most passionate during that time."[13]

Elvis's discharge from the army in early 1960 proved to be just as much of a media circus as his induction.

Journalists from around the world asked him many questions, including about his relationship with Priscilla.

"I'm very fond of her, but she's just a friend," Presley said. "There's no big romance."[14]

Elvis was not being fully truthful. In reality, the two had certainly had a romance going. Elvis and Priscilla had spent many evenings in his bedroom, talking and kissing. The night before he was to return to the United States, "I begged him to consummate our love," she later recalled. Elvis declined. He thought she was too young for that.[15]

On March 2, 1960, Elvis and Priscilla shared a tearful farewell before he boarded the plane back to the United States. He promised to call as soon as he got home. He even gave her his combat jacket as a token that she belonged to him.

Would Elvis still reign as the world's biggest rock and roll star? Or would his fans have moved on? He would soon find out.

8
Return to the Top

Elvis immediately realized that his fans had not forgotten him. If anything, his absence had made them appreciate him even more. When he reached Memphis, he needed a police escort to reach Graceland.

Within a couple of weeks, Elvis and his entourage traveled to Nashville, where he recorded a new single called "Stuck on You/Fame and Fortune" and four other songs for an upcoming album. To avoid an avalanche of fans, top-secret conditions prevailed.

Fans placed more than 1.2 million advance orders before the song had even been recorded. "Stuck on You," a mellow pop song, reached number one in less than a month and remained there for four weeks. The King of Rock and Roll had regained his crown.

Still, not all was rosy for Elvis. He strongly disapproved of his father's decision to marry Dee Stanley, whom Vernon had started dating in Germany. In fact, Elvis did not even attend the wedding. Vernon and Dee moved into Graceland along with Dee's three boys.

Elvis welcomed them as best he could, but his mind was focused on Hollywood. "More than anything, I want to be an actor," he said, "the kind that stays around for a long time."[1]

Making Bad Movies

Elvis got his wish—sort of. Producer Hal Wallis put Elvis right back to work in a movie called *G.I. Blues*. Critics criticized the plot and the song selection. Indeed, the film marked the beginning of a downward spiral for Elvis's film career. Over the next nine years, he made twenty-seven movies. Most were panned by movie critics, "but they were enormously popular—at least at first—as were the hit songs and albums that came from them.[2]

Some of his roles did give Elvis a chance to show his range as an actor. He really enjoyed his dramatic role as a nightclub singer in *King Creole*, and the movie still stands as one of his best. Likewise, he received praise for his role as a half-blood Kiowa in *Flaming Star*.

Other than *Jailhouse Rock*, many people consider *Viva Las Vegas* to be Elvis's best musical role. He had great chemistry with costar Ann-Margret, possibly because the two were dating in real life at the time. *Viva Las Vegas* ranked as the top-grossing film of Elvis's movie career, and it drew critical acclaim as well.

However, the overall quality of Elvis's movies declined as the decade of the 1960s wore on. Critic Pauline Kael summed it up this way: "He starred in thirty-one movies, which ranged from mediocre to putrid, and just about in that order."[3]

Another writer noted that Elvis's focus on movie making ended up "effectively sabotaging his previous career as a recording artist and live performer."[4]

Trying to Stay on Top

Still, Elvis remained a strong music presence—at least for awhile. In May 1960, he appeared on a Frank Sinatra

After a brief break from the spotlight, Elvis returned to prominence in 1960. That year he appeared on a television special with celebrity crooner Frank Sinatra.

television special. Parker demanded and got one hundred twenty-five thousand dollars for Elvis to appear on camera for just a few minutes. The show garnered huge ratings, but the critics were harsh. One said, "Although Elvis became a sergeant in the Army, as a singer he never left the awkward squad."[5]

Immediately after taping the Sinatra special, Elvis returned to Nashville. There, in one long session, he recorded the twelve songs for his *Elvis Is Back* album, which was released just a week later. Elvis aficionado John Robertson called it "the perfect Presley album" in that "it encapsulated within twelve songs everything that Elvis had been and meant during the Fifties and everything that he would become across the following decade."[6] The album mixed gritty blues, sizzling sensuality, and powerful pop sounds.

Unfortunately, most of his subsequent album releases in the 1960s failed to live up to this promise. Over the next eight years, RCA issued twenty-three Elvis Presley albums. Fifteen were movie soundtracks. Two more were compilations of previously recorded material. Only six represented original material.

None of these albums contained the raucous rock and roll for which he had first gained fame. Many featured a mix of ballads, pop, and soft rock. Elvis could still mesmerize listeners with his talented voice. Love songs such as "Are You Lonesome Tonight?" and "Can't Help Falling in Love" remain classics fifty years after their release.

Still, many fans believed he had lost the "edge" that had first launched him to stardom, and he no longer dominated the charts. Indeed, between "Good Luck Charm" in 1962 and "Suspicious Minds" in 1969 he went seven years without a number-one song.

Meanwhile, a new "generation" of musicians rose to the top in the early to mid-1960s. First and foremost were the Beatles, who launched a string of number-one hits that rivaled Elvis and who, for one magical week in April 1964, held all five top spots on *Billboard*'s charts. Still, if Elvis felt threatened by groups such as the Beatles, he didn't show it. In 1965 he invited the Beatles to visit him in California while they were doing an American tour.

"The Memphis Mafia"

From early on during his touring days, Elvis surrounded himself with a group of friends who traveled with him

"HEARTBREAK HOTEL"

The Beatles credit Elvis Presley with being one of their primary music influences. Beatle John Lennon said that "Heartbreak Hotel" was "the most exciting thing [we'd] ever heard. It was the spark, and then the whole world opened up for us." Elvis's record company had been unsure about releasing the song as a single. The somber melody and words did not sound like top-forty material. But Elvis knew the song was special. It sold two million copies and became his first national number-one hit. In many ways, "Heartbreak Hotel" typifies Elvis's early career. He selected excellent songs to record and delivered them with a styling that marked them as his own.

71

wherever he went. Over the years, as many as fifty different people were part of the group. Generally, however, he traveled with only a few at a time.

Some of the members included friends from high school, such as Red West and George Klein. West had once rescued Elvis from a gang of tough kids in high school, and he became Elvis's bodyguard.

Group members Charlie Hodge and Joe Esposito had become close friends with Elvis while serving in the army together. Hodge worked with Elvis for seventeen years, and Esposito served as the "foreman" of the entourage

Elvis's entourage earned the nickname "Memphis Mafia." Over time, their motto became "TCB," or "Taking Care of Business." That business involved catering to Elvis's needs at any hour of the day or night. Because of his strange sleeping habits, Elvis might wake up members of the group in the middle of the night to play racquetball, watch a movie, or even fly off to Las Vegas on a whim.

Members of the Memphis Mafia accompanied Elvis when he filmed movies. When he was home at Graceland, they stayed at or near his side. Some of them actually lived on the grounds of the estate.

Most of all, the people in his entourage were friends with whom Elvis could hang out and relax after a day of filming or a night of performing. For Elvis, wrote biographer Peter Guralnick, the Memphis Mafia represented "a group of guys with whom he could be comfortable and share some laughs and not have to worry about who he was or where he fit in."[7]

Elvis did not like to be alone. With the Memphis Mafia around, that was never a problem. Members of the entourage received a minimal salary, but all their expenses were covered. Plus, they got to mix and mingle

GENEROUS TO A FAULT

Elvis was famed for his generosity. Friends and even strangers might receive a car or financial help.

In addition, Elvis donated money to charities in Memphis. He also donated fifty thousand dollars to the Motion Picture Relief Fund. This fund helps needy people in the entertainment field. Elvis did charity concerts as well. Probably the most famous came in Hawaii in March 1961. Elvis performed before a crowd of fifty-five hundred people to raise money toward a memorial to recognize the USS _Arizona_. That battleship had been sunk during the Japanese attack on Pearl Harbor in 1941. The event raised more than fifty thousand dollars.[8]

with movie stars and stay in luxurious hotels. In addition, Elvis sometimes surprised them with gifts such as cars or gold jewelry. On more than one occasion, Elvis went on a car-buying binge in which he might buy a dozen or more cars and then give them to family members, his entourage, and other friends.

A True Ladies' Man

Talented. Handsome. Wealthy. Elvis ranked as one of the world's most eligible bachelors throughout 1960s.

Wherever he went, women threw themselves at him. Elvis did not hesitate to take advantage of these opportunities, even during times when he was dating someone he considered special.

Meanwhile, Elvis was linked with or actually dated several of his movie costars. Probably the most famous and most serious was Ann-Margret. Elvis starred with her in *Viva Las Vegas*. The two seemed perfectly suited to one another. In the end, however, "she fell short on Elvis' conviction that a wife should stay at home and not pursue a career," wrote Adam Victor.[9]

Through it all, Priscilla Beaulieu remained in Elvis's heart. For two years after returning home from Germany, he kept in touch sporadically. Then in mid-1962, he invited her to join him in California while he filmed a movie.

Priscilla's stepfather opposed this idea. However, Elvis assured Captain Beaulieu that seventeen-year-old Priscilla would be fully chaperoned during her entire visit. She promised that she would write home each day. As soon as she arrived, however, Elvis took her to Las Vegas. Before they left Hollywood, she pre-drafted a series of postcards. One of Elvis's friends mailed one each day, postmarked in Hollywood. That way, her parents would not be suspicious.

The visit went so well that Elvis invited her to spend the Christmas holidays in Memphis. After that visit, Elvis decided he couldn't live without Priscilla. He convinced her parents to let her attend school in Memphis. Elvis told Captain Beaulieu that Priscilla would live with Vernon and his new wife, Dee. In reality, she soon moved into Graceland with Elvis while she earned her high school diploma.

Meanwhile, drug use began to take a toll on Elvis. He took amphetamines to help him through the rigors of filming his movies and recording his albums. Then, struggling to sleep as he had for years, he took sleeping pills to slow down his body functions.

It may have been the drugs. It may have been the pressure. But those around him witnessed violent mood swings. They noticed "not just the loss of control but the absence of remorse in a nature that each of them saw as essentially soft-hearted, for good or for ill," wrote biographer Guralnick.[10]

Although she was only a teenager when they met, Elvis quickly became infatuated with Priscilla Beaulieu. She moved in with him at Graceland when she was only seventeen.

At the same time, Elvis also began to look for a deeper purpose in his life. His hairdresser, Larry Geller, convinced Elvis that the purpose in life is to discover the purpose of life. That idea moved Elvis, who often wondered why he had been chosen to become a superstar.[11]

Most pop artists remain popular for just a few years. By the mid-1960s it appeared that Elvis was beginning to slide. His songs no longer dominated the pop charts. His movies no longer dominated the box office.

In addition, he was beginning to lose some of his sex appeal. He had begun to put on weight. Growing up in poverty, Elvis did not have a wide choice of foods. When he became wealthy, he could have as much of whatever foods he wanted. The temptation proved more than he could handle.

At Graceland, there was a cook on duty twenty-four hours a day ready to prepare a meal whenever Elvis might be hungry. Elvis ate often, and he usually ate large portions. He enjoyed fried food and food prepared in rich buttery sauces. Over the years, his poor eating habits took a toll on both his digestive system and his heart.

On the occasion of his thirtieth birthday in 1965, *Time* magazine noted that "his second-skin jeans have been replaced by somewhat wider slacks."[12]

After nearly a decade at the top, was Elvis mania finally waning? Elvis managed to find ways to ensure that this would not happen.

9
Turning Things Around

J ust when it appeared that the King might be about to relinquish his crown, Elvis found ways to turn his life around, both personally and professionally.

In December 1966, he gave Priscilla Beaulieu a three-and-a-half-carat diamond engagement ring. Elvis said, "I told you I'd know when the time was right. Well, the time's right."[1]

Meanwhile, a new "partnership agreement" with Colonel Tom Parker went into effect at the beginning of 1967. The arrangement gave Parker a fifty-percent share in many aspects of Elvis's business.

Parker asked for this deal for several reasons. He feared the unpredictability of Elvis's fame and the increasing unpredictability of Elvis himself. "If he was going to tie his future and devote all of his considerable energies to one performer, there was little question in his mind that he should be getting some equity, too," wrote Elvis biographer Peter Guralnick.[2]

In February 1967, RCA released Elvis's religious album, *How Great Thou Art*. Although not an immediate hit, the album received much critical praise. It also earned Elvis his first Grammy Award, winning for "Best Sacred Performance." Grammy Awards are the top honors in the recording industry.

This album again demonstrated Elvis's ability to perform across genres. It also allowed him to return to his musical roots, singing the gospel music he had enjoyed so much as a young child.

The King Takes a Queen

Then, on the morning of May 1, 1967, one of the most eligible bachelors in the world went off the market. That day Elvis married Priscilla in Las Vegas. Colonel Parker made most of the arrangements. Only a handful of relatives and a couple of friends attended.

Elvis, a legendary ladies' man, met his match in Priscilla. After years of being accused of being a womanizer, Elvis tied the knot, marrying Priscilla on May 1, 1967, in Las Vegas, Nevada.

In fact, most of Elvis's entourage—his closest friends—
were not even invited. Many of them took this snub hard.
Red West even quit for two years. "The truth is, the suite
the ceremony was in was big enough for the rest of the
guys to be there," said Marty Lacker, who served as one of
two best men for the wedding. "But the Colonel invited
who he wanted."[3]

After the wedding, the bride and groom held a press
conference as reporters peppered them with questions.
"We appear calm," Elvis noted, "but Ed Sullivan didn't
scare me this much."[4] The newlyweds spent two days in
Palm Springs, and then flew back to Memphis. Later that
month, they held a reception at Graceland for friends,
relatives, and employees. For a while, they lived a peaceful
life as newlyweds.

"Sadly, the peace was not long lived," Priscilla later
recalled. "Forces he could not avoid—or chose not to
avoid—were calling him back."[5]

Indeed, his movie career continued slipping in
1967. Early in the year he filmed *Clambake*, one of his
least favorites among all his movies. He complained to
studio executives about the script, but no substantive
improvements were made.

"Elvis was so despondent over *Clambake* that his
weight ballooned from his usual 170 to 200 pounds by
the time he reported for work," Priscilla later recalled. To
get his weight back down, he resorted to diet pills.[6]

To make matters even worse, Elvis tripped in the
bathroom the day he was to report for filming. He
suffered a concussion, and production on the movie had
to be delayed.

About this time, Elvis met Dr. George Nichopoulos.
The two hit it off, and "Dr. Nick" went on to treat the

King's illnesses (and provide his prescription drugs) for the rest of Elvis's life. Although Elvis looked fit, in reality he was often under the influence of a variety of pills.[7]

Then something happened that caused Elvis to straighten out his life—at least for a while. In July, he announced to the press that Priscilla was pregnant. "This is the greatest thing that has ever happened to me," he said.[8]

Elvis's Comeback Special

In January 1968 the Colonel finalized a deal with NBC for Elvis to do a Christmas special—his first television appearance since 1960. Between the appearance and the

A LONG CAREER

Music trends change quickly. It takes talent, drive—and a bit of luck—to remain on top. That is why few performers are able to enjoy successful careers that span decades. There are exceptions, of course. The Rolling Stones and Beach Boys have remained popular touring groups for more than 50 years. Elvis Presley's career spanned three decades. He rose to prominence in the mid 1950s and remained a force until his death in 1977. One reason for his continued success was versatility. Over the years, he moved from rock and roll to ballads to gospel to a combination of the three in his 1970s performances.

film that would be made from the performance footage, Elvis would earn more than one million dollars.

Then, on February 1, 1968, Elvis became a father, as Priscilla gave birth to a baby girl. They named their daughter Lisa Marie. At first, family life seemed to suit Elvis. Whenever he was home, he doted on his daughter. Priscilla and Lisa Marie also spent time at a home that Elvis had bought in Los Angeles. That gave them a chance to spend more time together while Elvis filmed his movies.

Originally planned as strictly a Christmas special, Elvis's appearance on NBC later that year became an Elvis retrospective, with material spanning his career. The show revolved around the theme of a young man searching for happiness, with the song "Guitar Man" serving as a link to tie together the sequences. The idea of appearing live again energized Elvis, who spent about a month preparing for the show, which was taped at the end of June.

Elvis spent much of the summer filming a Western film called *Charro*. He enjoyed playing a dramatic role that was not built around singing. Still, he once again faced a mediocre script. *Variety* magazine summed it up by saying, "Elvis strolls through a role that would have driven any other actor up the wall."[9]

But Elvis took pride in the reaction to his television special. The show ranked as the number-one television show of the season.

Attired in a black leather outfit for parts of the show, Elvis looked like the Elvis of old. For this special, Elvis rocked. He crooned. He performed with the passion that had marked his rise to stardom in the 1950s. And the audience loved it.

Elvis admitted that the notion of taping in front of a live audience made him nervous. "For nearly ten years, I have been kept away from the public," he said. "And the one thing I loved was performing. But I'm not sure they're going to like me now."[10]

Elvis needn't have worried. Critics and fans alike loved his performance. The show became known as the "comeback special." It closed with the song "If I Can Dream," inspired by Martin Luther King, Jr.'s "I Have a

In the early years, only one girl could get between Elvis and Priscilla —their daughter, Lisa Marie, born on February 1, 1968.

Dream" speech. King had been assassinated in Memphis earlier in 1968. Elvis greatly admired King and had memorized King's famous speech.

Attired in a white suit and red tie, Elvis poured his heart and soul into performing this song, which offered a plea for peace and brotherhood. He closed with arms spread dramatically, and then uttered the words that impersonators have so often imitated: "Thank you. Thank you very much."[11]

Elvis's "comeback" continued to gather steam in January 1969. For his next album, he returned to Memphis, where he had recorded his first hits. One reason for his lackluster material during the 1960s rested with Parker's insistence that writers sign over a portion of the publishing rights for any song that Elvis recorded. Most top songwriters refused those terms. For this Memphis session, Elvis declared, "I don't care who owns it or what the deal is...I just want some great material."[12]

The Memphis sessions yielded two songs that ranked as all-time Elvis classics: "In the Ghetto" and "Suspicious Minds." "In the Ghetto" was a topical song about a poor young urban male who gets caught up in a life of crime and ends up dying. It probably reminded Elvis of his own poverty-stricken youth. The song reached number three.

"Suspicious Minds," meanwhile, became Elvis's first number-one hit in seven years. The song cemented the King's comeback, and it remained one of his favorite songs to perform in concert throughout the rest of his career. "An eternal tale of paranoia and deceit, it evidently struck a chord with Elvis, who heightened the tension of the verses and then poured out his heart," added John Robertson.[13]

The Memphis recording sessions also yielded the tracks for two albums: *From Elvis in Memphis* and *Back in Memphis*. The former is a true classic that The *Rolling Stone Album Guide* calls "one of the finest studio albums of his career."[14]

Amazingly, some fifteen years after bursting onto the scene, Elvis had reinvented himself. Moreover, he had finally completed his commitment to the grind of making movies. In his last film, *Change of Habit*, he played a

In June 1968, Elvis appeared on television in a comeback special. The success of the show, as well as his latest recordings, had inspired Elvis, and he found himself back on top once again.

doctor working in the slums of New York with a nun played by Mary Tyler Moore.

A Lavish Show in Las Vegas

The success of Elvis's television special and his latest recording sessions rekindled his passion for music. He decided that he wanted to return to singing live. The Colonel booked him to perform for four weeks at the brand-new International Hotel in Las Vegas.

The stage show Elvis put on was elaborate and lavish. He wanted to embrace all the types of music he had loved

ELVIS'S VEGAS SPECTACULAR

At 10:15 p.m. on opening night, August 1, 1969, the sellout crowd of two thousand rose to its feet and roared as Elvis strode onstage. Wearing a modified black karate suit, Elvis appeared as sexy and appealing as ever. He was described as "bursting with energy, falling to his knees, sliding across the stage, even doing somersaults."[15]

The invitation-only crowd, which included many celebrities and reporters, remained standing and cheering through most of the show. Highlights included a six-minute version of "Suspicious Minds" and his encore song, "Can't Help Falling in Love."

over the years. He assembled a cast of talented background singers and musicians, and he rehearsed diligently.

The audience loved the show. Critics did, too. "There are several unbelievable things about Elvis," said *Newsweek*, "but the most incredible is his staying power in a world where meteoric careers fade like shooting stars."[16]

Within hours after the performance, the Colonel met with the hotel management to extend the contract. Elvis was to receive one hundred twenty-five thousand dollars a week for two four-week engagements a year through 1974. This came to one million a year for just eight weeks work.

Amazingly, the decade of the 1960s ended just as it began—with Elvis Presley standing as the King of Rock 'n' Roll. Furthermore, he appeared poised to extend his reign into the 1970s as well. Sadly, it was not to be.

10

Caught in a Trap

In "Suspicious Minds," Elvis Presley sang about being "caught in a trap." In many ways, that summed up his life as the 1970s began. At first glance, everything seemed great. Elvis rode a huge wave of popularity, and his latest records were hits. His performances in Las Vegas had drawn rave reviews.

But Elvis still faced many of the same challenges that had dragged down his career during much of the 1960s. His rigorous schedule of moviemaking was immediately replaced with a series of energy-draining live performances. To cope, he once again turned to drugs—amphetamines to help him get up for performances, sleeping pills to help him wind down, and diet pills to help keep off weight.

In February 1970, Elvis made four historic appearances at the Houston Astrodome, which seated around 45,000 people. At the first show, he was discouraged by poor acoustics, and a luke-warm reaction from a less-than-capacity crowd. By the second show, however, both he and the audience had regained their enthusiasm. At the evening show on the second day, 43,614 fans attended.

In April, his song "The Wonder of You" was released, reaching number nine on the charts. In June, Elvis spent several days recording in Nashville, focusing on country-and-western songs.

August found Elvis back in Las Vegas. Once again audiences went wild at the sold-out shows. Footage from these performances formed the basis for the documentary film *That's the Way It Is*.

In early September, Elvis embarked on a brief tour—his first real tour since 1957. It went so well that another tour immediately followed. Colonel Tom Parker saw touring as a surefire way to generate income—lots of income.

Elvis's hectic schedule took its toll on his family life. When Elvis Presley first began doing his Las Vegas engagements, Priscilla and Lisa Marie visited frequently. When they were apart, Priscilla sent Elvis daily "care packages" of photos and tape recordings of his little girl.

Over time, however, Priscilla found that Elvis's renewed popularity began to drive a wedge between them. "Thriving on all the excitement, glamour, and hysteria, he found it difficult to go home and resume his role as father and husband," she later wrote.[1]

In November 1970, Elvis admitted to the press that his marriage was "going through a difficult patch."[2]

Guns and a White House Visit

Elvis collected guns for years. In the 1970s, his collection numbered thirty-eight weapons, including an assault rifle, a submachine gun, and gold-plated pistols.

Elvis's fixation with guns led to an amazing meeting. In December 1970, after arguing with his father and Priscilla over expenses (including money spent on guns), he flew to Washington, D.C., on a whim. Once there, he sought a meeting with President Richard Nixon.

Elvis wanted Nixon to give him a federal narcotics officer's badge. Although not an Elvis fan, the conservative Nixon agreed to meet the wild singer with his open shirt and gold jewelry.

Elvis offered to help Nixon in the war against illegal drugs in the United States by delivering an antidrug message to young people. This may seem ironic in light of Elvis's own dependence on pills. Elvis, however, did not consider his pills "drugs" because they were prescribed.

In the end, Elvis received both a badge and a photo identification card from the U.S. Department of Justice.

LOSING HIS QUEEN

Celebrity marriages are always difficult. Life in the constant spotlight puts strain on even the strongest celebrity relationships. That's one reason why the divorce rate among rock stars, actors, and sports stars is so high. Before Elvis married Priscilla on May 1, 1967, he was arguably the world's most eligible bachelor. The King (and his Queen) ranked among the world's best-known megacouples. Elvis truly loved Priscilla, but he was easily (and often) tempted by the many women he met while on concert tours or shooting movies. His marriage to Priscilla lasted six years. Many factors contributed to the decline of Elvis's career and health in the 1970s, but his break-up with Priscilla was certainly one of the main ones.

"Elvis believed that this badge gave him the authority to carry guns and whatever pharmaceuticals he wanted anywhere in the country," wrote Adam Victor.[3]

Living Legend

Still in the prime of his career, Elvis had already become a living legend. In June 1971 his birthplace in Tupelo, Mississippi, opened for tours to the public. Around the same time, a long stretch of Highway 51 South, part of

In December 1970, Elvis took an impromptu trip to Washington, DC, to meet with President Richard Nixon and volunteer his services as a special undercover narcotics officer to keep youths off drugs.

which runs in front of Graceland, was officially renamed Elvis Presley Boulevard.

In the summer of 1971, Elvis received the Bing Crosby Award from the National Academy of Recording Arts and Sciences. This special recognition is given for lifetime achievement, and Elvis received it at the age of thirty-six.

Elvis capped his professional year with a successful tour of a dozen cities in the fall. His outfits grew more elaborate, his glittery black or white jumpsuit now accompanied by a matching cape.

A Marriage in Crisis

All of these accomplishments, however, were overshadowed by the disintegration of Elvis's marriage in 1971. His constant inattention and womanizing finally grew too much for Priscilla to endure.

Ironically, karate played a role in the breakup. Priscilla started her training so that she and Elvis would have an activity to share. She trained with karate expert Mike Stone. The training increased her self-confidence and lessened her dependence on Elvis. She longed for a more normal life.

Also, Priscilla found herself falling in love with Stone. When Priscilla told Elvis she was leaving, he asked if he had lost her to another man. "It's not that you've lost me to another man," she replied. "You've lost me to a life of my own. I'm finding myself for the first time."[4]

Priscilla and Lisa Marie left Graceland on December 30, 1971. Elvis's friend Jerry Schilling recalls that after they left, Elvis shut himself in his bedroom and cried. "That was the beginning of the end for the Elvis I had known and loved," Schilling said.[5]

A Red-Hot Hit

At first Elvis kept moving forward as if nothing had happened. In 1972, Elvis continued to perform in Las Vegas and Lake Tahoe. In March and April, MGM filmed Elvis in a recording and on tour. The resulting film, *Elvis on Tour*, won a Golden Globe award for Best Documentary. In April, he released a gospel album titled *He Touched Me*, which won a Grammy Award.

In June 1972, Elvis performed at four sold-out shows at New York's famed Madison Square Garden. The star-studded audience went wild, and *Time* magazine hailed his comeback as "perhaps the most impressive in the history of pop music."[6]

BURNING LOVE

"Burning Love" proved to be the last top-ten single of Elvis's life. However, Elvis continued to place songs on the country charts during the 1970s. Over his career, he recorded hits that spanned from rock to country, from rhythm and blues to gospel. His versatility and longevity stand as hallmarks of his career. In 2002, decades after his death, a remix of his song "A Little Less Conversation" became a hit thanks to its inclusion on the album *ELV1S: 30 #1 Hits*. Even though he was no longer around to enjoy his success, he had proven once again that he was and always would be the King.

Meanwhile, Elvis's latest single, "Burning Love," was just about to burn up the airwaves. This energetic song was the first true rock-and-roll song he had released in some time, and it captured some of the old magic of his early days in music.

Although Elvis did not like the song, it reached number two on the Billboard charts.

Following his split with Priscilla, Elvis had a steady stream of women. Then in July 1972, he met Memphis State University student Linda Thompson, the reigning Miss Tennessee. They began a four-and-a-half-year relationship. Seemingly bolstered by his new romance, Elvis dove into preparations for another historic event—a live show that would be beamed by satellite all over the world.

On January 14, 1973, more than one billion people worldwide watched live as Elvis performed in Honolulu, Hawaii. "This is Elvis at his most iconic," said one review, "the Elvis his impersonators would aspire to become."[7]

A Downward Spiral

Soon after Elvis's triumphant satellite performance, however, things began to go wrong. He once again began to put on weight, and his use of pills increased. Although audiences still enjoyed his shows, the critics blasted Elvis. "The Living Legend is fat and ludicrously aping his former self," wrote the *Hollywood Reporter.*[8]

In September, Elvis got into a bitter argument with Colonel Parker and fired his long-time manager. That lasted until the Colonel presented a detailed accounting of money he claimed Elvis owed him. In the end, Elvis backed down.

Although Elvis and Priscilla were in the midst of a divorce when this photo was taken in 1973, they remained on good terms, leaving the courthouse arm in arm.

Meanwhile, the divorce between Elvis and Priscilla became final in 1973. The agreement called for joint custody of Lisa Marie, and she continued to visit Elvis regularly. Elvis spoiled Lisa Marie, buying her a pony and her own golf cart to ride around Graceland.

Just a week after the divorce, Elvis went into a Memphis hospital due to breathing problems. He remained there for more than two weeks. Doctors identified several problems, including his dependence on prescription drugs.

In 1974, Elvis continued to do his Las Vegas shows and tour across the country, but the quality of his performances from show to show varied widely. *Life*'s book *Remembering Elvis: 30 Years Later* described his concerts this way: "Attending an Elvis concert in the '70s was like rolling the dice in a Vegas casino: anything from a jackpot to a crap-out was possible."[9]

In April 1975 came an offer that could have turned Elvis's life around. Actress Barbra Streisand's production company offered Elvis a role in her forthcoming movie *A Star Is Born*. The movie, which depicts a classic Hollywood tale of success and failure, would provide a perfect vehicle for Elvis to revive his film career. The deal fell through when Parker demanded a higher salary than the producers were willing to offer.

Throughout the rest of 1975 and 1976, Elvis continued to tour and perform, with his performances becoming increasingly erratic. His personal behavior became more erratic, too, and he spent money wildly.

The year 1976 also was marked by personnel problems. Bodyguards Sonny West and Red West had caused several lawsuits to be brought against Elvis after they used excessive force in dealing with unruly fans. In July,

Vernon fired them, along with Dave Hebler, in what he termed a cost-cutting measure.

Deeply offended, the Wests and Hebler began preparing a tell-all book titled *Elvis: What Happened?* (told to writer Steve Dunleavy), which detailed Elvis's drug use and other erratic behavior. In October 1976, Linda Thompson left as well. She could no longer handle the constant attention and pampering that Elvis required.

Although Elvis immediately found another girlfriend, nineteen-year-old Ginger Alden, it was clear that his support system was falling apart. Still, he rallied to give a spirited New Year's performance in Pittsburgh, Pennsylvania.

11

The Death of the King

Could the King turn things around yet again? Sadly, no. In January 1977, Elvis failed to show up for a scheduled recording session in Nashville.

Colonel Tom Parker, panicking after Elvis missed the recording session, brought Dr. Nick in to keep a close eye on Elvis's drug intake.

Elvis tried to rouse his spirits by proposing to Ginger Alden. He gave her a ring featuring the eleven-and-a-half-carat diamond out of his own Taking Care of Business (TCB) ring. The two did not set a wedding date.

Elvis did one brief tour in February and another in March. On March 30, he stumbled through songs. He even changed the lyrics to his classic song "Can't Help Falling in Love" from "Wise men say/Only fools rush in" to "Wise men know/When it's time to go." Was it an accident, or was Elvis foreseeing an end to his career?[1]

On March 31, 1977, Elvis grew so ill that he had to cancel the final few dates of his tour. That day, too, he learned the tell-all book by Red West, Sonny West, and Dave Hebler was coming out that summer. Elvis worried how his fans would react to revelations about his drug use and behavior with women. He was even more concerned about what his father and daughter would think.

When he got home from his tour at the beginning of April, Elvis checked into a hospital in Memphis. Discharged after a few days, he went home to Graceland to rest.

A Disastrous Tour

Within three weeks, however, he began yet another tour. To keep him company, he brought Ginger along. The tour was disastrous. Comments from reviewers and fans included such notes as "seeming not to care" and "he stunk."[2] A writer in Detroit summed it up this way: "At best, he is a parody of himself."[3]

Two upcoming shows were being filmed for a television special. Concerned about how he would look on-screen, Elvis took diet pills on top of the pain pills, amphetamines, and sleeping pills he already took. The performance in Omaha was a disaster, but he rallied for the show in Rapid City. "He looked healthier, seemed to have lost a little weight, and sounded better, too," wrote biographer Peter Guralnick.[4]

When that tour ended, Elvis went home to Graceland. As the publication date for the book that his former entourage members had written drew closer, he worried about how the book would affect his already declining career. He had even more trouble than usual sleeping.

Final Days

Lisa Marie Presley arrived on July 31 for a visit. Elvis rented out Libertyland, a local theme park, after hours one evening. The group of about twenty stayed all night. "His friends remember him as a proud father, somewhat solemn but fun loving as he accompanied her from ride to ride with the other children and adults he had invited to go with him," wrote biographer Jerry Hopkins.[5]

Elvis planned to depart on August 16 for a brief, ten-city tour. At 10:30 p.m. on August 15, he had a dentist's appointment with Dr. Hofman, who cleaned his teeth and filled a couple of small cavities. Elvis returned to Graceland shortly after midnight and went directly upstairs.

Four months before he died, Elvis was photographed during a performance in Milwaukee, Wisconsin. Though he was no longer a heartthrob, he still drew crowds with his melodious voice.

That night Elvis and Ginger talked about the upcoming tour. They talked about marriage, and Elvis even said he might announce it at the Memphis concert at the end of the tour.

At 2:15 a.m. on August 16, Elvis called Dr. Nick and said that one of his new fillings was bothering him. Dr. Nick prescribed some pain medication, and a member of Elvis's entourage picked up the pills at an all-night pharmacy. A couple of hours later, Elvis called his cousin Billy Smith to play some racquetball. They played for only a few minutes before Elvis grew tired. He went back inside and sang at the piano for a few minutes before going back upstairs.

Soon after that, he took the first of three packets of prescription drugs that he used to help him sleep. A couple of hours later he was still awake, so he took the second packet. Later he took the third and told Ginger he was going into the bathroom to read.

Ginger awoke around 1:30 p.m. on August 16. Soon after, she opened the bathroom door and found Elvis lying on the floor. His face lay in a pool of vomit on the thick shag carpet. She immediately called for help. Members of Elvis's entourage rushed upstairs, but there was nothing they could do.

Meanwhile, young Lisa Marie came to the bathroom door and saw her father on the floor. "My daddy's dead! My daddy's dead!" she cried.[6]

An ambulance rushed Elvis to Baptist Memorial Hospital in Memphis. Efforts to revive him continued, but at 3:30 p.m., he was pronounced dead. An autopsy began at 7:00 p.m., but even before it was completed, the press was informed that Elvis died of "cardiac arrhythmia." In other words, he had had a heart attack.[7]

Meanwhile, members of Elvis's entourage had to inform Priscilla, Vernon, and Colonel Parker that Elvis had died. Parker then had to handle all the details of canceling the tour.

Stunned Reactions

News of Elvis's death spread quickly. By the next day, an estimated fifty thousand had gathered at Graceland. From 3:00 to 6:30 p.m., mourners filed by the copper coffin, paying their tribute to the King. People came from all over the United States. Priscilla flew in from California to mourn her former husband and comfort her daughter.

ELVIS'S FINAL SECRETS

The results of Elvis's autopsy remained private. This led to rumors about his death that have lasted for years. People have wondered whether Elvis committed suicide or could have been killed. Some, basing their ideas on tabloid stories, have claimed that Elvis was, in fact, still alive.

Lab reports filed two months later described fourteen different drugs in Elvis's system at the time of his death. Ten of those drugs were present in significant quantities. Taken together, they could easily have caused a lethal overdose.

SUDDEN DEATH

The life of a rock and roll star takes its toll. The grind of recording and performing is relentless. Elvis Presley is part of a long list of famous music performers who saw their lives end during what should have been their prime years. Others include Janis Joplin, Jimi Hendrix, Michael Jackson, Prince, Whitney Houston, John Lennon, Buddy Holly, Alliyah, Bob Marley, Tupac, and Selena, as well as many more. Some died of drug and alcohol-related problems. A few were murdered. Some died in airplane crashes. Marley died of cancer. Some, however, have gone on to live (and perform) into their seventies and beyond.

Even in the days before internet, within hours people across the world heard the news on television or radio. Many remembered their experiences listening to Elvis's music.

Meanwhile, newspaper headlines across the world proclaimed his death. In Russia, a newspaper ran a full-page about Elvis's death. It simply said, "Elvis is dead. The USA has given us three cultural phenomenon: Mickey Mouse, Coke a Cola (sic), and Elvis Presley." In Britain the front page read, "King Elvis Dead at 42 and Alone."[8]

Even in death, Elvis was surrounded by a media circus. On August 18, a brief service was held at Graceland.

Memphis Press-Scimitar

U.S. WEATHER FORECAST: A 60 per cent chance of rain with high in the upper 80s. Low tonight low 70s. High Thursday mid 80s.

97TH YEAR   MEMPHIS, TENN., WEDNESDAY, AUGUST 17, 1977   TELEPHONES: NEWS and GENERAL 526-2141 CIRCULATION 525-7801 WANT ADS 526-8892

SPECIAL EDITION

Memphis Leads the World in Mourning the Monarch of Rock 'n Roll

A Lonely Life Ends on Elvis Presley Boulevard

By CLARK PORTEOUS
Press-Scimitar Staff Writer
(Aug. 17,1977)

The King is dead.

Elvis Presley — the jiggling, jiving, rock 'n roll king — lived just 42 years, seven months and eight days.

It was an exciting but frustrating life which ended in Baptist Hospital, where Elvis was pronounced dead at 3:30 p.m. yesterday of a heart attack.

Elvis made millions of dollars and literally was worshiped by millions of fans. But he was lonesome much of the time, paid a high price for privacy and could not do many things he would have liked to do because he always drew a crowd of admirers.

Elvis, with a pleasant singing voice and a new style, strumming a guitar and gyrating his pelvis — which brought him the name in early days of "Elvis the Pelvis" — made millions, was able to buy anything he wanted, yet happiness seemed to elude him.

Elvis gave away countless thousands, giving funds to numerous Memphis institutions just before Christmas every year. He would give his friends — and occasionally even strangers — expensive automobiles.

Yet as the years passed, many of his friends seemed to have faded away, not generally because they wanted to, but some said Elvis had changed.

Elvis Aron Presley was written about on his 40th birthday, and friends were quoted as saying he was "fat and forty" and refused to see anybody until his weight got down to his regular trim 180 pounds. He was staying in his mansion, Graceland, on Elvis Presley Boulevard, a part of Bellevue renamed by city fathers to honor Elvis.

He became more and more of a recluse in his last few years. Red West and other close friends, who used to be called the "Memphis Mafia," were no longer with him.

Elvis, already a living legend and somewhat of a folk hero to many, was found unconscious at Graceland at 2:30 p.m. yesterday.

Maurice Elliott, Baptist Hospital vice president, said Joe Esposito, Presley's road manager and long-time friend, was

A Tribute to Elvis

The unexpected death of rock 'n roll star Elvis Presley Aug. 16, 1977, was news of international impact. Almost every news agency in the world reported the tragedy under a Memphis dateline.

The public interest required that many members of The Press-Scimitar staff have a hand in compiling and presenting the story. Every conceivable angle was covered in a period of five publication days. Requests for copies of The Press-Scimitar containing coverage of the singer's death poured in from all over the world in great numbers. It was impossible to meet the demand.

Therefore, as a public service to its readers, The Press-Scimitar has reprinted in this special tribute edition all Elvis Presley stories and pictures published in the five-day period. With as few changes as possible, all stories and pictures that we published in the regular editions of The Press-Scimitar are reprinted herein. This edition plus a similar edition of The Commercial Appeal are offered to readers for 50 cents.

"Goodby, darling, goodby — I loved you so much," a sobbing Elvis said before leaving the burial site. "I lived my whole life just for you."

Elvis once recalled that in his boyhood his mother was very possessive of him, probably due to the loss of the twin. The Presleys had no other children.

"My mama never let me out of her sight," Elvis said. "I couldn't go down to the creek with the other kids. Sometimes, when I was little, I used to run off. Mama would whip me and I thought she didn't love me."

Elvis knew extreme poverty as well as extreme wealth.

His father, Vernon, who has shared in his son's success, did odd jobs and farmed in Tupelo, but the family was poor. When Elvis was 14, the family moved to Memphis. They lived in a one-room apartment on Alabama in North Memphis at first, later moved into Lauderdale Courts, one of the two first public housing projects built

Elvis was graduated from Humes in 1953. He had been too small to make the football team, but he was interested in sports and learned to be an expert at karate.

After graduation from Humes, Elvis worked on the assembly line of a precision tool company, then at a furniture factory making plastic tables and then as a truck driver for Crown Electric Co. He also ushered at Loew's State, a theater which was later to show many of his movies.

In the summer of 1953, Elvis took the step which led to fame and fortune. He had "just an urgin'" and went to Sam Phillips' Sun Record Co. He paid to have a recording made for his mother. Elvis said "it sounded like somebody beating on a bucket lid." But Elvis was told he had an unusual voice and someone might call him.

Months passed and Elvis kept driving a truck for $35 a week. At night he attended a trade school, studying to be an electri-

ELVIS PRESLEY: THE BEAT WENT ON — AND ON AND ON

— UPI Telephoto

Mourners In Waiting For Last Homecoming Of Revered Singer

By CHARLES GOODMAN

the crowd, which had surged forward. A

Elvis passed away from a heart attack on August 16, 1977. The morning after, his death was front-page news across the country as fans and friends mourned the loss of the King.

Then the body was carried to Forest Hill Cemetery in a white hearse, followed by seventeen white limousines. A brief ceremony followed. Then Elvis was laid in a white marble mausoleum, near where his mother was buried. Within two months, however, both Elvis and Gladys were reburied at Graceland.

The King was dead. But his memory and music remained.

CONCLUSION

Elvis has been dead for more than forty years. But his legend lives on through his music and movies.

Elvis remains big business, even in death. In 2015, his estate generated $55 million. This ranked only behind Michael Jackson as the top-grossing dead celebrity, according to *Forbes* magazine. The income comes from Graceland visitors, CDs, and DVDs.

Elvis's will named his father as executor and trustee of his will. Beneficiaries were his grandmother, Minnie Mae Presley, who still lived at Graceland, his father, and Lisa Marie Presley. Vernon Presley left most of his affairs in the hands of Parker.

When Vernon died in 1979, control of Elvis's estate passed to Priscilla. She broke off from Parker, which led to several years of court battles.

For a while, it appeared that Priscilla might have to sell it. It simply cost too much to keep it running. Still, Priscilla did not want Lisa Marie to "grow up and have regrets that everything had been sold."

Then someone suggested that Graceland be opened to the public. Graceland opened on May 4, 1982. " "I think he'd be very pleased to know that the house is shown in this way," Priscilla said.

More than 600,000 people visit Graceland each year. Only the first floor is open to the public. This includes the music room, the dining room, the TV room, the billiard room, the kitchen, and the den, which is also named the "jungle room" because of its décor. The Hall of Gold in Elvis's trophy building is lined with his gold and platinum albums. The hall pays tribute to his sales of more than one billion records worldwide, more than any other entertainer in history.

Lisa Marie followed in her father's footsteps by launching a career as a recording artist. However, she is probably best known for her brief marriage to another famous singer—Michael Jackson. The two were married

A fan shows off her impressive collection of Elvis memorabilia in 1988. Though he's been dead for more than four decades, Elvis albums and souvenirs continue to sell to fans old and new.

Lisa Marie Presley followed in her famous father's footsteps, recording and releasing three full-length albums of her own music between 2003 and 2012.

from 1994 to 1996. During much of the 1980s, Jackson ranked as the most popular singer in the world. Known as the "King of Pop," Jackson had in some ways taken over Elvis's spot. Like Elvis, he died young.

But, most of all, Elvis lives on through his music. At any moment of the day or night, an Elvis song is probably playing somewhere in the world. Furthermore, hundreds of Elvis tribute artists keep the King's memory alive with live performances.

Elvis's songs and his influence have stood the test of time. According to *Livewire*, Elvis Presley ranks number seven on the list of top ten most influential rock artists of all time. In 1986, Elvis was among the first inductees into the Rock and Roll Hall of Fame in Cleveland, Ohio. In 1992 and 2015, his image appeared on a US postage stamp.

The Elvis legacy lives on through all the other artists he has influenced. These include the Beatles, Rolling Stones, Led Zeppelin, and Bob Dylan, noted *Livewire*. Fellow Rock and Roll Hall of Fame member Bruce Springsteen once hopped the fence at Graceland in hopes of meeting his idol. Elvis was not home, and his security guards escorted Springsteen back out to the street.

How influential was Elvis Presley? He dominated music and films. He influenced generations of pop/rock musicians. He became the first celebrity so famous he needed only a single name—Elvis. He was, and remains, the King!

CHRONOLOGY

Elvis Aaron Presley is born on January 8 in Tupelo, Mississippi; his twin brother, Jesse Garon, is born dead.

A tornado tears through Tupelo, killing more than two hundred people, it destroys the church across the street from the Presleys, but leaves their house untouched.

Elvis's father, Vernon, is sent to prison for illegally altering the amount on a check.

The Presley family briefly moves to Pascagoula, Mississippi; they stay only a few months.

Elvis starts first grade in 1941; the United States enters World War II in December following the Japanese attack on the U.S. naval base at Pearl Harbor, Hawaii.

Sings at a talent show at the annual Mississippi-Alabama Fair and Dairy Show, winning fifth place.

Gets his first guitar and soon begins taking it to school.

The Presley family moves to Memphis, Tennessee.

Enters Humes High School and stands out because of his long, slicked-back hair and colorful clothing.

Wins the senior class variety show with his singing; graduates from high school on June 3, the first member of his immediate family to earn a diploma; pays four dollars to record two songs to give to his mother as a present.

108

1954 Begins dating Dixie Locke; called in to Sun Studio to record; releases his first record, "That's All Right," which becomes a hit; performs his first concert.

1955 Begins touring; becomes a regular at the popular *Louisiana Hayride*; signs with RCA records after RCA buys his contract from Sun.

1956 Breaks through on the national scene with four number-one hit records, including the classics "Heartbreak Hotel" and "Hound Dog"; signs management contract with Colonel Tom Parker; performs on several national television shows, including *The Ed Sullivan Show*; makes his first movie, *Love Me Tender*.

1957 Releases four more number-one songs and two more hit movies, including *Jailhouse Rock*.

1958 Is inducted into U.S. Army; his mother, Gladys, dies; he is shipped out to Germany; his popular movie *King Creole* is released.

1959 Serves successfully in the army; becomes involved romantically with fourteen-year-old Priscilla Beaulieu.

1960 Completes service in the army and returns to United States; releases more hit albums and songs; stars in *GI Blues* and *Flaming Star* movies.

1961-1965 Continues to release strings of albums, singles, and movies, which gradually begin to lose commercial appeal; Priscilla Beaulieu comes to Memphis in 1963 to finish high school and moves into Graceland.

Proposes to Priscilla just before Christmas.

Purchases the Circle G ranch in Mississippi; releases gospel album *How Great Thou Art*, which wins a Grammy Award; marries Priscilla on May 1.

Welcomes birth of daughter, Lisa Marie, on February 1; performs in a television special that relaunches his career.

Films his last theatrical movie, *Change of Habit*; releases "In the Ghetto" and "Suspicious Minds," his two hottest songs in years; the latter becomes his first number-one hit in seven years; performs in wildly successful stage shows in Las Vegas.

Launches first tour since 1957; stars in documentary film *That's the Way It Is*; meets President Richard Nixon.

Continues to tour and perform in Las Vegas; sets attendance records at the Houston Astrodome; receives lifetime achievement award from the National Academy of Recording Arts and Sciences.

Releases gospel album *He Touched Me*, for which he receives his second Grammy; sells out Madison Square Garden for four shows; separates from Priscilla and begins dating Linda Thompson.

Performs in *Aloha from Hawaii*, a special concert beamed live via satellite around the world and viewed by more than a billion people; receives a Golden Globe for the *Elvis on Tour* documentary filmed a year earlier;

signs new recording contract with RCA and new management contract with Colonel Parker; finalizes divorce from Priscilla.

Concert tours and Las Vegas shows continue, but the quality is variable and Elvis's health begins to decline.

Records his last single, "Way Down"; breaks up with Linda Thompson and begins dating Ginger Alden.

Tours early in year but experiences increasing health problems; dies on August 16 just prior to launching another tour.

Vernon Presley dies of a heart attack.

Graceland opens to the public.

Elvis is among the first inductees into the Rock and Roll Hall of Fame.

Elvis's image appears on a postage stamp.

CHAPTER NOTES

Introduction

1. Peter Guralnick, *Last Train to Memphis: The Rise of Elvis Presley* (Boston: Little, Brown, 1994), p. 338.

2. Jennifer Rosenberg, "1956—Elvis Gyrates on Ed Sullivan's Show," About.com, n.d., http://history1900s.about.com/od/1950s/qt/el vissullivan.htm (accessed June 1, 2009).

3. Glenn C. Altschuler, *All Shook Up: How Rock 'N' Roll Changed America* (New York: Oxford University Press, 2003), pp. 90–91.

4. Fred Bronson, *The Billboard Book of Number 1 Hits* (New York: Billboard Books, 2003), p. 10.

5. Guralnick, p. 311.

6. Adam Victor, *The Elvis Encyclopedia* (New York: Overlook Duckworth, Peter Mayer Publishers, Inc., 2008), p. 370.

7. Peter Guralnick and Ernst Jorgensen, *Elvis Day By Day: The Definitive Record of His Life and Music* (New York: Ballantine Books, 1999), p. 95.

8. Rosenberg.

9. Altschuler, p. 91.

Chapter 1: A Legend Is Born

1. Alanna Nash, *Elvis Aaron Presley: Revelations From the Memphis Mafia* (New York: HarperCollins, 1995), p. 9.

2. Jerry Hopkins, *Elvis: The Biography* (London: Plexus, 2007), p. 21.

3. Peter Guralnick, *Last Train to Memphis: The Rise of Elvis Presley* (Boston: Little, Brown and Company, 1994), p. 13.

4. Gene Smiley, "Great Depression," *Library of Economics and Liberty*, n.d., http://www.econlib.org/ library/Enc/ GreatDepression.html (accessed June 1, 2009).

5. Elaine Dundy, *Elvis and Gladys* (New York: Macmillan, 1985), p. 57.

6. Ibid., p. 58.

7. Larry Geller and Joel Spector with Patricia Romanowski, *"If I Can Dream": Elvis' Own Story* (New York: Avon Books, 1989), p. 30.

8. Paul Simpson, *The Rough Guide to Elvis* (London: Rough Guides Ltd., 2004), p. 9.

Chapter 2: Musical Beginnings

1. Elaine Dundy, *Elvis and Gladys* (New York: Macmillan, 1985), p. 93.

2. Peter Guralnick, *Last Train to Memphis: The Rise of Elvis Presley* (Boston, Little, Brown, 1994), p. 21.

3. Ibid., p. 17.

4. Larry Geller and Joel Spector with Patricia Romanowski, *"If I Can Dream": Elvis' Own Story* (New York: Avon Books, 1989), p. 31.

5. Guralnick, p. 18.

6. Ibid.

7. Paul Simpson, *The Rough Guide to Elvis* (London: Rough Guides Ltd., 2004), p. 11.

8. Dundy, p. 101.

9. Guralnick, p. 19.

10. Ibid.

11. Ibid., pp. 19–20.

12. Adam Victor, *The Elvis Dictionary* (New York: Overlook Duckworth, Peter Mayer Publishers, Inc., 2008), p. 84.

Chapter 3: A New Life in Memphis

1. Jerry Hopkins, *Elvis: The Biography* (London: Plexus, 2007), p. 28.

2. Peter Guralnick, *Last Train to Memphis: The Rise of Elvis Presley* (Boston: Little, Brown and Company, 1994), p. 36.

3. Paul Simpson, *The Rough Guide to Elvis* (London: Rough Guides Ltd., 2004), p. 419.

4. Elaine Dundy, *Elvis and Gladys* (New York: Macmillan, 1985), p. 139.

5. Guralnick, p. 45.

6. Peter Guralnick and Ernst Jorgensen, *Elvis Day By Day: The Definitive Record of His Life and Music* (New York: Ballantine Books, 1999), p. 12.

Chapter 4: Starting on the Road to Success

1. "What Things Cost: Prices for 1954," The Fifties Web, n.d., http://www.fiftiesweb.com/pop/prices- 1954.htm (accessed June 12, 2009).

2. Jerry Hopkins, *Elvis: The Biography* (London: Plexus Publishing Limited, 2007), p. 40.

3. Helen Clutton, *Everything Elvis: Fantastic Facts About the King* (London: Virgin Books Ltd., 2004), p. 6.

4. Adam Victor, *The Elvis Encyclopedia* (New York: Overlook Duckworth, Peter Mayer Publishers, Inc., 2008), p. 308.

5. Peter Guralnick, *Last Train to Memphis: The Rise of Elvis Presley* (New York: Little, Brown, 1994), p. 80.

6. Ibid.

7. Paul Simpson, *The Rough Guide to Elvis* (London: Rough Guides Ltd., 2004), p. 18.

8. Elaine Dundy, *Elvis and Gladys* (New York: Macmillan, 1985), p. 179.

9. Peter Guralnick and Ernst Jorgensen, *Elvis Day By Day: The Definitive Record of His Life and Music* (New York: Ballantine Publishing Group, 1999), p. 19.

10. Robert Sullivan, ed., *Remembering Elvis 30 Years Later* (New York: Life Books, 2007), p. 18.

11. Ibid.

12. Ibid., pp. 129–130.

13. Ibid.

Chapter 5: Becoming the King

1. Peter Guralnick and Ernst Jorgensen, *Elvis Day By Day: The Definitive Record of His Life and Music* (New York: Ballantine Books, 1999), p. 27.

2. Alanna Nash, *The Colonel: The Extraordinary Story of Colonel Tom Parker and Elvis Presley* (Chicago: Chicago Review Press, 2004), p. 119.

3. Ibid., p. 185.

4. Ibid., p. 74.

5. Peter Guralnick, *Last Train to Memphis: The Rise of Elvis Presley* (Boston: Little, Brown and Company, 1994), p. 233.

6. Guralnick and Jorgensen, p. 54.

7. Ibid., p. 53.

8. Ibid., p. 81.

9. Glenn C. Altschuler, *All Shook Up: How Rock 'n' Roll Changed America* (New York: Oxford University Press, 2003), p. 89.

10. Adam Victor, *The Elvis Encyclopedia* (New York: Overlook Duckworth, Peter Mayer Publishers, 2008), p. 370.

11. Guralnick, pp. 285–286.

12. Helen Clutton, *Everything Elvis: Fantastic Facts About the King* (London: Virgin Books Ltd., 2004), p. 16.

13. Loanne M. Parker, "Colonel Tom Parker," Rockabilly Hall of Fame, n.d., http://www.rockabillyhall.com/ColTom.html (accessed June 14, 2009).

14. Nash, p. 119.

Chapter 6: On His Throne

1. Adam Victor, *The Elvis Encyclopedia* (New York: Overlook Duckworth, Peter Mayer Publishers, 2008), p. 318.

2. Jerry Hopkins, *Elvis: The Biography* (London: Plexus Publishing, 2007), p. 122.

3. Victor, p. 269.

4. "National Average Wage Index," Social Security Online, October 16, 2008, http://www.ssa.gov/OACT/COLA/AWI.html (accessed February 6, 2009).

5. Elaine Dundy, *Elvis and Gladys* (New York: Macmillan, 1985), p. 293.

6. Peter Guralnick, *Last Train to Memphis: The Rise of Elvis Presley* (Boston: Little, Brown, 1994), p. 417.

7. Robert Palmer, *Rock & Roll: An Unruly History* (New York: Harmony Books, 1995), p. 51.

8. Guralnick, p. 440.

9. Ibid., p. 441.

10. Ibid., p. 294.

11. Robert Sullivan, ed., *Remembering Elvis: 30 Years Later* (New York: Life Books, 2007), p. 70.

12. Alanna Nash, *The Colonel: The Extraordinary Story of Colonel Tom Parker and Elvis Presley* (Chicago: Chicago Review Press, 2003), p. 175.

13. Hopkins, p. 128.

14. Ibid.

Chapter 7: Serving His Country

1. Jerry Hopkins, *Elvis: The Biography* (London: Plexus, 2007), pp. 134–135.

2. Ibid., p. 135.

3. "Elvis Presley Graceland + Army Induction," Elvis Presley Music, n.d., http://www.elvispresleymusic .com.au/pictures/1958_march_24.html (accessed February 26, 2009).

4. Alanna Nash with Billy Smith, Marty Lacker, and Lamar Fike, *Elvis Aaron Presley: Revelations from the Memphis Mafia* (New York: HarperCollins, 1995), p. 131.

5. Marie Clayton, *Elvis: The Illustrated Biography* (Croxley Green, U.K.: Transatlantic Press, 2008), p. 87.

6. Larry Geller and Joel Spector with Patricia Romanowski, *"If I Can Dream": Elvis' Own Story* (New York: Avon, 1989), p. 38.

7. Robert Sullivan, ed., *Remembering Elvis: 30 Years Later* (New York: Life Books, 2007), p. 80.

8. Peter Guralnick and Ernst Jorgensen, *Elvis Day By Day: The Definitive Record of His Life and Music* (New York: Ballantine Books, 1999), p. 126.

9. Andreas Schroer, *Private Presley* (New York: William and Morrow, 1993), p. 49.

10. Ibid., p. 140.

11. Hopkins, p. 149.

12. Peter Guralnick, *Careless Love: The Unmaking of Elvis Presley* (Boston: Little, Brown and Company, 1999), p. 41.

13. Hopkins, p. 153.

14. Schroer, p. 153.

15. Sullivan, p. 87.

Chapter 8: Return to the Top

1. Robert Sullivan, ed., *Remembering Elvis: 30 Years Later* (New York: Life Books, 2007), p. 90.

2. Paul Simpson, *The Rough Guide to Elvis* (London: Rough Guides Ltd., 2004), pp. 305–306.

3. Pauline Kael, "This Is Elvis," The Niuean Pop Cultural Archive, n.d., http://www.unknown.nu/misc/ elvis.html (accessed February 28, 2009).

4. John Robertson, *Elvis Presley: The Complete Guide to His Music* (London: Omnibus Books, 2004), p. 34.

5. Jerry Hopkins, *Elvis: The Biography* (London: Plexus, 2007), p. 159.

6. Robertson, p. 49.

7. Ibid., p. 50.

8. Peter Guralnick, *Careless Love: The Unmaking of Elvis Presley* (Boston: Little, Brown and Company, 1999), p. 68.

9. Peter Harry Brown and Pat H. Broeske, *Down at the End of Lonely Street: The Life and Death of Elvis Presley* (New York: Dutton, 1997), p. 237.

10. Adam Victor, *The Elvis Encyclopedia* (New York: Overlook Duckworth, Peter Mayer Publishers, 2008), p. 467.

11. Guralnick, p. 87.

12. Larry Geller and Joel Spector with Patricia Romanowski, *"If I Can Dream": Elvis' Own Story* (New York: Avon Books, 1989), p. 23.

Chapter 9: Turning Things Around

1. Priscilla Presley, *Elvis and Me* (New York: G.P. Putnam's Sons, 1985), p. 222.

2. Ibid., p. 216.

3. Peter Guralnick, *Careless Love: The Unmaking of Elvis Presley* (Boston: Little, Brown and Company, 1999), p. 249.

4. Alanna Nash with Billy Smith, Marty Lacker, and Lamar Fike, *Elvis Aaron Presley: Revelations from the Memphis Mafia* (New York: HarperCollins, 1995), p. 432.

5. Jerry Hopkins, *Elvis: The Biography* (London: Plexus Publishing, 2007), p. 199.

6. David Ritz, ed., *Elvis by the Presleys* (New York: Crown, 2005), p. 130.

7. Presley, p. 231.

8. Peter Harry Brown and Pat H. Broeske, *Down at the End of Lonely Street: The Life and Death of Elvis Presley* (New York: Dutton, 1997), p. 310.

9. Peter Guralnick and Ernst Jorgensen, *Elvis Day By Day: The Definitive Record of His Life and Music* (New York: Ballantine Books, 1999), p. 232.

10. Paul Simpson, *The Rough Guide to Elvis* (London: Rough Guides Ltd., 2004), p. 358.

11. Robert Sullivan, ed., *Remembering Elvis: 30 Years Later* (New York: Life Books, 2007), p. 109.

12. "Elvis Presley—If I Can Dream," YouTube, http://www.youtube.com/watch?v=mfvsepvgCCc& feature=PlayList&p=C391FC681B2C64F4&playnext =1&playnext_from=PL&index=17.

13. Simpson, p. 118.

14. Toby Creswell, *1001 Songs: The Great Songs of All Time* (New York: Thunder Mouth's Press, 2006), p. 453.

15. John Robertson, *Elvis Presley: The Complete Guide to His Music* (London: Omnibus Books, 2004), p. 64.

16. Anthony DeCurtis and James Henke, eds., with Holly George-Warren, *The Rolling Stone Album Guide* (New York: Random House, 1992), p. 556.

Chapter 10: Caught in a Trap

1. Peter Guralnick and Ernst Jorgensen, *Elvis Day By Day: The Definitive Record of His Life and Music* (New York: Ballantine Books, 1999), p. 269.

2. Priscilla Presley, *Elvis and Me* (New York: G.P. Putnam's Sons, 1985), p. 277.

3. Marie Clayton, *Elvis: The Illustrated Biography* (Croxley Green, U.K.: Transatlantic Press, 2008), p. 179.

4. Adam Victor, *The Elvis Encyclopedia* (New York: Overlook Duckworth, Peter Mayer Publishers, Inc., 2008), p. 405.

5. Presley, p. 300.

6. Paul Simpson, *The Rough Guide to Elvis* (London: Rough Guides Ltd., 2004), p. 47.

7. Peter Harry Brown and Pat H. Broeske, *Down at the End of Lonely Street: The Life and Death of Elvis Presley* (New York: Dutton, 1997), p. 361.

8. David Ritz, ed., *Elvis by the Presleys* (New York: Crown, 2005), p. 163.

9. Robert Sullivan, ed., *Remembering Elvis: 30 Years Later* (New York: Life Books, 2007), p. 112.

Chapter 11: The Death of the King

1. Peter Guralnick, *Careless Love: The Unmaking of Elvis Presley* (Boston: Little, Brown and Company, 1999), p. 628.

2. Peter Guralnick and Ernst Jorgensen, *Elvis Day By Day: The Definitive Record of His Life and Music* (New York: Ballantine Books, 1999), p. 372.

3. Jerry Hopkins, *Elvis: The Biography* (London: Plexus Publishing, 2007), p. 367.

4. Guralnick, p. 638.

5. Hopkins, p. 376.

6. Ibid., p. 380.

7. Guralnick and Jorgensen, p. 379.

8. Guralnick, p. 649.

amphetamine A type of drug that stimulates the nervous system.

artifact An object that relates to a person, time, or place.

aspire To hope for or plan for.

audition To try out for.

blatant Obvious, often in a loud or rude manner.

bloated Swollen or puffed up.

chronic Continuing for a long time; having long had a disease or other health problem.

debut Appearing or doing something for the first time.

deferment Temporary postponement for entering military service.

demeaning Degrading, embarrassing.

disquiet A state of anxiety or uneasiness.

draft To be required to serve in the military based on selection in a lottery system.

endorsement A recommendation of something or someone.

entourage A group of attendants, usually associated with a person of importance.

eviction To expel, especially as in making someone leave a building, usually through a legal process.

foreshadow To indicate or suggest something before it happens.

furlough A vacation or leave of absence from military service.

going steady An old-fashioned term for dating.

gold record A song or album that has sold 500,000 copies or downloads.

grossing Earning. A top-grossing record is one that has earned the most money from sales.

gyrations Movements in a circular or spiral motion.

icon A symbol or image that represents something.

inducted Admitted as a member, especially into military service.

jailbird A person who has served time in jail.

jaundice A condition in which the skin is yellowed, usually because of a disease.

mesmerize To fascinate or hold spellbound.

munitions Materials used in war, especially weapons and ammunition.

number-one song A song that has reached the top of the sales charts and has received a significant amount of attention from radio stations.

oblivion The state of being forgotten or unknown.

platinum record A song or album that has sold a million copies or downloads.

prophecy A prediction of the future.

putrid Of low quality; rotten.

ravishing Extremely beautiful.

rendition A version or translation of something.

renowned Well known, famous.

secluded Private, sheltered from public activity.

sharecropper A tenant farmer who pays as rent a share of the crop.

sporadic Occasional, happening at irregular intervals.

svelte Slender.

venue A site or place where an event takes place.

vindicated Upheld or justified.

FURTHER READING

Books

Alden, Ginger. *Elvis and Ginger: Elvis Presley's Fiancee and Last Love Finally Tells Her Story.* New York, NY: Berkley, 2015.

Chanoinat, Philippe and Fabrice Le Henanff. *Elvis.* New York, NY: NBM Graphic Novels, 2015.

Connolly, Ray. *Being Elvis: A Lonely Life.* New York, NY: W.W. Norton & Company, 2017.

Freedland, Michael. *Elvis Memories: The Real Presley — By Those Who Knew Him.* London, UK: The Robson Press, 2014.

Wertheimer, Alfred and Peter Guralnick. *Elvis: A King in the Making.* New York, NY: Chartwell Books, 2017.

Websites

Elvis Presley Official Website

www.elvis.com

The official website for Elvis Presley, including biographical and discographical information, as well as photos of the King.

Elvis News

www.elvisnews.com

The leading news site for information about Elvis, including news about new releases, as well as information on his life.

Graceland

www.graceland.com

Elvis's famous home in Memphis, Tennessee, the Graceland website includes information on Elvis's life as well as his hometown.

Films

Elvis 75th Birthday Collection. 20th Century Fox, 2010.

Johnson, Liza. *Elvis & Nixon.* Sony, 2016.

Klug, Rob. *Elvis by the Presleys.* BMG, 2005.

Sanders, Denis. *Elvis: That's the Way It Is.* WarnerBrothers, 2014.

INDEX